THE
GRADUATE'S
BOOK OF
PRACTICAL
WISDOM

To Misha Tinney —
Best wishes for your best life !

June 2009

To Julia Teena —

Best wishes for your best life.

[signature]

June 2009

THE
GRADUATE'S
BOOK OF
PRACTICAL
WISDOM

99 Lessons
They Can't Teach
in School

C. Andrew Millard

New York

The Graduate's Book of Practical Wisdom

99 Lessons They Can't Teach In School

ISBN 978-1-60037-558-3

Library of Congress Control Number: 2008944264

MORGAN · JAMES
THE ENTREPRENEURIAL PUBLISHER

Morgan James Publishing, LLC
1225 Franklin Ave., STE 325
Garden City, NY 11530-1693
Toll Free 800-485-4943
www.MorganJamesPublishing.com

In an effort to support local communities, raise awareness and funds, Morgan James Publishing donates one percent of all book sales for the life of each book to Habitat for Humanity. Get involved today, visit **www.HelpHabitatForHumanity.org**.

For my son Drew,

who embodies everything a father would want in a son.

Contents

part three   PERSONAL RELATIONSHIPS

Acknowledgments.

The transition from youth to adulthood forces us to look backward and ahead at the same time. Who we are at any given point in time is an accumulation of all the experiences we have had up to that point. The same can be said of a book such as this.

Just like you, I grew up being influenced by many people, some of whom were central to my daily life and others who have been forgotten. Each one contributed an important piece to the puzzle that eventually became the adult. In a very real sense, those people have contributed to this book by shaping the experiences that inform the lessons. It is not possible to recognize them all, just as you will never be able to adequately thank everyone who helped make you the person you are.

Nevertheless, I would like to take a moment to recognize some people who have had a more or less direct influence upon the book you hold in your hands. First on the list is my family, especially my parents and grandparents, who taught me many of the lessons I pass along here. My wife, brother and sisters also have been great sources of strength and support.

My son Drew, to whom this book is dedicated, was the direct inspiration for it. He was the unwilling object of all my advice for several years, challenging my concepts and causing me to sharpen my arguments into something that would be meaningful to a clever twenty-first century young adult. He was also my most effective editor.

Others who contributed their ideas, critiques and edits included: Sharon Millard, Betsy Goree, Carroll Brady, Tracey Daniels, Juliet Botescu and Katie Norton. I also wish to thank David Hancock and his entire team at Morgan James Publishing for their confidence, creativity, professionalism and support.

This is clearly a short and inadequate list, and there are many other names that belong on it; but the limitations of space and memory have kept it short. To those I have omitted, please accept my apologies and gratitude.

You only live once—but if you work it right, once is enough.

—Joe E. Lewis

Introduction:
How you can benefit from this book.

Life will teach you all this stuff eventually. The more you pick up now, the better off you'll be.

They say that youth is wasted on the young. Being young yourself, you can't really know what this means yet, so I'll tell you. Right now, you have three things going for you: (1) time, (2) energy, and (3) a belief that you can change the world. As a young adult, you enter a world of limitless possibilities, and you think you're ready for anything. In some ways you are, and in some you're not.

There's a downside to youth: your pool of life experience is limited to a few short, childhood-era years. But as each day passes, you become just a bit smarter than you were the day before. Over a long period of months and years— and later, decades—you become vastly advanced from your previous self.

Some days, you learn more than others. Some days— usually days involving a very tough experience—you learn more than you want to learn. But one thing's for sure: you're just starting out in life. Although the possibilities are indeed limitless, you still have a *lot* to learn.

I'm sure you realize that there are some things they just don't teach you in school. What they *do* teach is knowledge. What they *can't* teach is wisdom. And a happy life takes just as much wisdom as it does knowledge—in fact, more.

You may have noticed that the words *wise* and *old* are often used together. That's because wisdom generally takes a long time to acquire. The downside of old age, of course, is that by the time you become old and wise, all that time and energy you had as a youth are in short supply.

The idea of this book is to help you gain as much practical wisdom as possible *now*—to give you a head start in life, so to speak.

And there's one thing I can guarantee: the wiser you are, the happier and more successful you will be.

part one

the basics

If you don't like something, change it. If you can't change it, change your attitude. Don't complain.

—Maya Angelou

Lesson 1:
Attitude is *everything.*

If you get nothing else from this book, get this:

Your attitude is *the* prime factor in some of the most important things in your life: personal happiness, success in your career, the quality of personal relationships, effectiveness in getting what you want, ability to deal with problems, and how others view you.

Adults have lectured you about your attitude since you were a kid. Let's take a fresh look at what's rightly been called "the magic word."

For the record, Houghton Mifflin's *American Heritage Steadman's Medical Dictionary* defines *attitude* as: "A relatively stable and enduring predisposition to behave or react in a certain way."

Think about the phrase "relatively stable." Your attitude doesn't change with each situation. It generally holds true wherever you are and whatever you're doing.

This next bit is one of life's greatest lessons, elegant in its sheer truth and simplicity:

A great attitude will result in a great life.

A lousy attitude will result in a lousy life.

You have *complete and total control* over your own attitude, so choose wisely.

The single greatest thing you can do for yourself is to adopt and keep a positive attitude about everything in your life. Wouldn't you rather enjoy life than trudge through each day with a dark cloud over your head, dreading the next hour, wishing for something you can't define? You can have that good life. You just have to make the decision, and then put it into practice every day.

Studies have shown that the one trait that's always present in highly successful people is—you guessed it—a great attitude.

Almost all of the lessons in this book relate in some way or other to this one. Burn it into your subconscious. Believe it. Live it, and you cannot fail.

There is nothing either good or bad,
but thinking makes it so.

—William Shakespeare

Lesson 2:
It's all in your head.

Early on, we must establish the premise that *you, and only you, have control over your own thinking.* This is an absolute truth, and you must accept it before going further.

To reject this premise is to view yourself as helpless, weak, and unable to think independently. Everyone knows on some level that they can control their minds, but most never consciously *do* it. Once you accept that you can control your thinking, the next step is to *take responsibility* for doing so.

Have you ever known anyone who only seemed to be happy when he or she was miserable? This may be because you can blame misery on someone else, but you must take personal responsibility in order to be happy. As Robert Anthony put it, "Most people would rather be certain they're miserable than risk being happy."

What these miserable people can't grasp is that their misery is their own fault, just as they would deserve the credit if they were happy. Both happiness and misery are results of simple decisions you make about your attitude.

Martha Washington said, "The greater part of our happiness or misery depends on our dispositions, and not on our circumstances." Follow this logic with me for a moment: if our happiness is determined by our disposition, and we can control that disposition, then *we have the power to create our own happiness.*

Your disposition is like a garden: if you pay attention to it and give it care, it will grow and flourish. If you ignore or neglect it, then weeds will creep in, the good stuff will die, and it will get ugly.

You are the gardener of your own disposition. It's not a job that you can delegate to others, and it's not going to happen on its own. If it's going to get done, you will have to do it yourself. Don't expect outside forces to provide that which you alone control.

All I'm asking of you right now is that you accept that you can control your own thinking and resolve to do so. Resolve—here and now—that you will not leave your own disposition to chance. Take responsibility for the kind of person you will be.

Scientists are generally happier than artists,
since they're commonly lost in objective tasks
and not examining their own navels.

—Bertrand Russell

Lesson 3:
It's not really about you.

One of the great ironies of life is that the only way to be personally fulfilled is to place your focus outside of yourself.

Consider the sad cases of any number of celebrities and professional athletes. Paris Hilton. Britney Spears. Lindsay Lohan. Marilyn Monroe. Judy Garland. Michael Jackson. Michael Vick. O.J. Simpson. The list goes on and on and on.

What does this unfortunate but diverse group have in common? From a very early age, they were taught that they were special. All parents try to instill this thought in their children, but in these cases there was no accompanying sense of humility, no understanding of their need to fit into and improve the world around them. These young people were so special that the normal rules of behavior and obligation did not apply. Their goal in life was to show the world how beautiful, talented, and special they were, not to make a contribution to society.

In short, it was all about them.

I don't know about you, but I have always felt deeply sorry for these sad individuals. What a miserable existence it must be to spend one's entire life in the vacuum of self. But they are smart people; they must instinctively have known that this was not right, even though their so-called friends assured them that it was. Too often, the ironic result of this conflict is secret, agonizing insecurity and a futile search for meaning.

What does this have to do with you? Children are naturally and unavoidably self-centered creatures, and adults, in an effort to instill self-esteem, often magnify this mindset through their words and actions. As you approached adulthood yourself, you most likely came to realize that the world does not actually revolve around you. In that respect, you're already several steps ahead of the group we've been discussing.

But here's the kicker: true happiness, real fulfillment, and successful personal relationships can only be achieved when you shift your focus *from* yourself *to* others. That's not to say that you should ignore or deny the things that make you special—quite the opposite. Cherish and develop them. Use those gifts to make a positive impact on the world around you. That is the way to real self-esteem.

Nobody really cares if you're miserable,
so you might as well be happy.

—Cynthia Nelms

Lesson 4:
Happiness is a permanent condition.

Let's clarify the difference between happiness and gladness. Gladness is a temporary feeling brought on by some good event or circumstance. Happiness is a *permanent state of mind* that remains unaffected by events or circumstances.

You were *glad* when you graduated from college or high school. You'd be *glad*—thrilled—if you won the lottery. Even something as momentous as the birth of a child causes gladness, but not happiness. As important as all these events are, they are circumstances—things which happen to or around you. They do not have the power to make you happy or unhappy. That power rests with you alone.

It's quite simple, really. We *create our own* happiness by what we think and do. Earl Nightingale put it this way: "Happiness is a by-product of something else. It comes from the direction in which we're moving." This sentiment is in perfect accord with Martha Washington's notion that happiness depends on our dispositions rather than our circumstances.

In other words, if you seek happiness directly, you'll surely fail. It comes as a result of (1) making a decision to be a happy person, and (2) living the kind of worthwhile, useful life that leads to happiness.

Easier said than done? Not really. We've already established that you control both your decisions and your behavior.

I'm not asking you to become a different person—far from it. You are uniquely you, and that fact should be celebrated. But you're not the *exact* same person today that you were at ten years old, are you? You've even changed some in the past year or two, right? And you'll continue to evolve as you work your way through adulthood.

Most important, make the decision to consciously direct your own thinking and attitude. As you go through this book, let the lessons soak in. As you incorporate them into your daily living, I suspect that over time your behavior may change as well. After all, your behavior is bound to evolve over the years anyway, is it not? Why not exercise control over that change in a way that benefits you and those around you?

*A great obstacle to happiness is to
anticipate too great a happiness.*

—Fontenelle

Lesson 5:
Don't look forward to happiness; live it now.

A young man I know moved with his family from a large northern city to a small southern town during the summer before his senior year in high school. Such a move would be a tough challenge for any young person, but it was especially hard on David. He had been happy and involved in his previous school, with lots of friends and activities. Now he was starting his senior year in an unfamiliar environment. He had no friends and found himself surrounded by a whole culture that was foreign to him. Sometimes, listening to the local accent and regional slang, he even had trouble understanding the language.

As you might imagine, David was wretchedly unhappy. He knew he'd be unhappy even before the move. The one thought that sustained him was his plan to move himself back to his old hometown immediately after graduation. He just knew that if he could get back home, everything would be fine again.

Graduation came and went. David packed some stuff in an old van, said goodbye to his parents, and pointed north. Once he got there, he got a job and settled into an apartment with a longtime friend as a roommate. And guess what? That's right; he was still miserable.

Here's an even more extreme example: Matt made a similar move just before his senior year. He moved from an even larger city—in France, no less—to tiny town in rural North Carolina. And Matt came alone, with no family and just a basic grasp of the English language. But far from being unhappy, Matt had a great senior year. He made lots of friends and got involved in many activities. The return to his home at the end of the year was bittersweet.

You see, David made several mistakes. First, he had a negative attitude about the move south. Second, he didn't adapt to his new surroundings. Third, he thought that his happiness depended on his circumstances. And Matt? Well, Matt was an exchange student. He *wanted* to be there. As a result, his attitude was positive, he adapted quickly, and he relished the unfamiliar surroundings.

Decide to be happy *now*, in this moment, regardless of the circumstances. Don't fool yourself into thinking that happiness will come later, once certain conditions are met. It won't. Remember: happiness doesn't come to you. You must create it within yourself.

When I was a child, I spoke as a child,
I felt as a child, I thought as a child.
Now that I have become a man,
I have put away childish things.

—1 Corinthians 13:11

World English Bible

Lesson 6:
It's time to take responsibility.

In almost every state, once you reach the age of eighteen, you're legally on your own. In the eyes of the law, you're totally responsible for—and held accountable for—your own actions.

That fact frequently causes indignation in eighteen year olds. It most often takes the form of the old cliché "I'm old enough to die for my country, but I'm too young to buy a beer."

Fair or not, that's the way it is. And the sooner you embrace responsibility, the happier you'll be. Being a responsible person is not a burden to be avoided. On the contrary, you now have the complete ability to determine the direction of your own life.

The idea of being a responsible adult is probably the greatest opportunity of your young life, but it comes at a price. We've already touched on the upside: you're now your own person. You can live where and how you want, do whatever you want (as long as it's legal), and do what you want with your life.

Now for the cost. It's just the flip side of the same coin. You now have nobody but yourself to blame for almost everything. You—and only you—are responsible for every single aspect of your own life.

Actions have consequences; even inaction has consequences. It's the price you pay to be in the game. Nothing's free. You can do—or not do—just about anything you want. Just be willing to pay the price. As soon as you understand how the game works, you can make it work for you. You'll wear responsibility as comfortably as the clothes on your back.

Many people never accept this simple concept, and as a result they are miserable until the day they die. They live what Thoreau called "lives of quiet desperation." All the while, they blame cruel fate, cruel people, or a cruel world for their misery. They'd rather be unhappy than face the fact that they live in a world of their own making.

Don't let that happen to you. Don't blame anyone for your troubles—not even yourself. Take responsibility for the kind of person you will be, for creating your own life. You'll find that—far from being a burden—responsibility is one of the secrets to a lifetime of happiness.

Beliefs constitute the basic stratum, that which lies deepest, in the architecture of our life. By them we live, and by the same token we rarely think of them.

—José Ortega y Gasset

Lesson 7:
Have a set of values and live by them.

Your values serve as your internal compass. They guide your actions. When you find yourself in a situation where you're unsure of what to do, your personal belief system will tell you what is right to guide your actions.

This compass will be vitally important in countless situations throughout your life, especially when you find yourself under pressure. If you have a hard-wired set of values, you'll be more likely to act in a way that you'll be proud of afterwards.

In order to reap those benefits later, however, you have to take some time now to define for yourself what your values are.

You already have a set of values; you just need to clarify them in your own mind. Your values have been influenced over the years by your parents, teachers, mentors, role models, and friends. But while others have a hand in the process, your values must be your own—nobody else's.

Fred "Mr. Rogers" Rogers once wrote, "I doubt that we can ever successfully impose values or attitudes or behaviors on children—certainly not by threat, guilt, or punishment." That also holds true for adults, but it has never stopped people from trying—just human nature, I guess.

So the challenge for you as a new adult is to separate the beliefs that belong to others from those that are really your own. Use your best adult judgment and try to sort through your own biases. Just as it doesn't make sense to simply accept your parents' values without testing them for yourself, it also doesn't make sense to blindly reject those values out of youthful rebelliousness or a desire for independence.

If you believe something to be true, then it doesn't matter where you first heard it. If it's true, it's true. Just make sure you can reconcile that truth in your own mind.

Understand also that your values and beliefs are likely to evolve over the years. But once you are clear about what you believe, you will find that the answers to tough questions will come much more easily.

Too soon old, too late smart.

—Old Pennsylvania Dutch saying

Lesson 8:
Time flies—even when you're not having fun.

This is not a complicated concept, but it's deep, and most people never wake up to it until late in life.

The great philosopher Ferris Bueller once said, "Life moves pretty fast. If you don't stop and look around once in a while, you could miss it." Truer words were never spoken. Life speeds by in the blink of an eye, and the older you get, the faster it seems to go.

In what will seem like two weeks, you're going to be old. I don't mean two weeks older than you are now; I mean old. Even as you read the words on this page, you are hurtling inescapably toward old age. Short of dying early, there's nothing you can do to stop the process.

Most young people don't really understand that today's old fuddy-duddies are yesterday's young punks. The reverse, of course, is that you are tomorrow's old fuddy-duddy. Between now and then, you'll probably have a series of jobs and eventually retire; possibly marry and have children and grandchildren of your own; make a fortune and probably spend most of it; and experience great excitement, great boredom, great joy, and great anguish.

In short, what happens between now and old age is the great adventure of life. Relish it, savor it, enjoy every moment. Imagine the things you'll learn, the wisdom you'll gain, the lives you'll touch with each passing day and year. And the process doesn't stop once you reach old age; the adventure continues until your final breath.

But there's another secret here that you shouldn't miss. The process of growing old is the process of living, which is to say that it is a wonderful and glorious process. It follows, then, that being old is not a thing to dread, but a badge of honor for a life well spent. It also follows that those who are old now have a lot to teach you.

You know that time flies. You know that it seems to go faster with each passing year. Each moment is precious; use it well. As Gandalf said in Tolkien's *The Fellowship of the Ring*, "All we have to decide is what to do with the time that's given to us."

Decide wisely.

Do to others as you would have them do to you.

—Christianity: Luke 6:31

*Hurt not others in ways that you
yourself would find hurtful.*

—Buddhism: Udana-Varga 5:18

*Do not do to others what you do not
want them to do to you.*

—Confucianism: Analects 15:23

*None of you [truly] believes until he wishes for
his brother what he wishes for himself.*

—Islam: Number 13 of Imam,

"Al-Nawawi's Forty Hadiths."

...Thou shalt love thy neighbor as thyself.

—Judaism: Leviticus 19:18

Lesson 9:
The Golden Rule works.

Every major world religion contains a version of what we call the Golden Rule. Just take a glance at the quotes above, and you'll get an idea of how universal this concept is. There's a reason for this: it *works*.

Let's be honest: we do everything—and I mean everything—to serve our own self-interest. That's not a bad thing; it's the way we are wired, the way nature intended it. And it's what makes the Golden Rule so perfect.

You know exactly how you would like to be treated. You know how it feels to be treated with respect. You know the kind of service you want in a restaurant, the loyalty you want from your friends, the kind of love you want from your family. In every aspect of life, you have a picture of how you'd like to have others "do unto you."

Now, just reverse the roles. Put yourself in that other person's place. It's a strikingly simple concept—even a schoolchild can understand it—but it's a decidedly grown-up thing to actually pull off. It doesn't work for kids because they are virtually incapable of placing another person's needs above their own. Adults, on the other hand, have the maturity to make this noble leap—although some never do.

Here's where your own self-interest comes in. Just because you know how you'd like to be treated and are capable of putting yourself in another person's moccasins, that doesn't mean that you automatically treat others in the way you'd like to be treated. You might have to give up a hard-earned advantage, take partial blame for something you feel is not your fault, or be nice to a person you don't really like. In order for you to live the Golden Rule all the time, it would have to be clearly in your best interest to do so.

It is. By treating your fellow humans as you wish to be treated, you increase your own chances of establishing and maintaining healthy relationships, whether it be a fifty-year marriage to your soul mate or a thirty-minute encounter with a waitress at a lunch counter.

So, take that leap. Give up an advantage now and then. Accept the blame. Be nice to that person you can't stand. The rewards will come back to you as surely as a boomerang does. Believe it, and it will happen.

To carry a grudge is like being stung to death by one bee.
—William Walton

Lesson 10:
Forgive, for your own sake.

Without a doubt, there will be many times in your life when others will do you wrong in some way or other. Some of these wrongs will be accidental, others deliberate. Some will be monsters—life-changers that will hurt deeply and cause major heartaches.

The people who commit these wrongs will be as varied as the acts themselves. Coworkers, friends, relatives—there's no telling where hurtful events can originate. The most painful source is close family members—a parent, spouse, or sibling. Worst of all, you yourself may be the source of an unspeakable action that hurts those you love.

Forgive. As hard as it is, forgive. Forgive everyone. Forgive them for every wrong.

Most important, forgive yourself. Until you forgive, you can't truly move forward. And you must move forward.

Your life lies in the future, not the past. Don't let the past hold you back. There's nothing you can do about the past—it's gone, and you can never bring it back. The only time period you have any control over is the time that's ahead.

Going back and rehashing past wrongs is a frustrating, useless exercise that does nobody any good. It's like picking at a scab. The way to heal a wound is to leave it alone and let time and nature do their work.

What is forgiveness? It is a genuine, deep-down, permanent release from any harsh feelings, resentment, or anger. You've heard people say, "I can forgive, but I can't forget." Well, that's not really forgiveness at all. Forgive and forget. It's not easy, but you must do it—for your own sake as well as others'.

It's true: carrying a grudge really is like being stung to death by a single bee. What's more, these are self-inflicted wounds; the person carrying the grudge keeps stinging himself.

Forgiveness carries the tremendous power to heal and to liberate at the same time. Stop stinging yourself. Forgive, and get on with your life. And when you are wronged in the future, forgive again, and again, and again. Leave the past behind, and keep moving ahead.

Freedom lies in being bold.

—Robert Frost

Lesson 11:
Be bold.

When my sister Nancy was about thirteen, our mother took her on a trip to Washington, DC to see the monuments and visit the museums. One museum housed a temporary exhibit of rocks that had been collected by astronauts during a NASA moon mission. Nancy and Mom saved this exhibit for the last day of their trip.

When they arrived at the exhibit hall, they were met with a sign that read "Moon Rock Exhibit Temporarily Closed." My sister was deeply disappointed; this was to have been the highlight of the trip. But my mother was not to be denied. She made it clear that she had come to see the moon rocks, and she was going in, regardless of the sign.

"Mom!" Nancy protested. "Can't you read? You'll get in trouble; you might get arrested!" It made no difference. Mom strolled past the sign and into the deserted hall. A few minutes later, Nancy was horrified to see her mother being escorted out by a burly security guard who politely but firmly reminded the little lady that the exhibit was closed.

"See?" Nancy said. "I told you you'd get in trouble!"

"Well," Mom replied with a quiet smile. "I saw the moon rocks."

Get the point? My mom was bold, and she was successful in her quest. My sister held back, and she didn't get to see the moon rocks.

Have you ever heard someone say, "I should have done so-and-so?" Boldness will keep you from ever having to say that.

You can express boldness in every aspect of your life, whether it be big or small. If you want to do something—as long as it's legal and worthwhile—do it. If you want a different job or a graduate degree, make up your mind to go for it. If you're in a karaoke club and want to sing, then sing! If you care about someone, don't be afraid to express how you feel.

Live the life that you want to live. Don't be held back by some notion that you aren't good enough, or that you might fail or be embarrassed. Don't let fear keep you from doing what you want to do.

Be bold, my friend, and you will never have to live with regret.

The really happy person is one who can
enjoy the scenery when on a detour.

—Unknown

Lesson 12:
Be flexible—to a point.

When I was in graduate school, a professor gave me a criticism which I took to be a backhanded compliment. "The problem with you, young man," he said, "is that you're always trying to change the rules to suit you."

Obviously, we can't always change the rules to our liking. The fact that we don't agree with something doesn't mean we can ignore it. You may think the speed limit is unreasonably low on a certain road, but if you speed on that road, you'll still get a ticket. Many, many circumstances are totally beyond your ability to direct. Your success or failure under those circumstances will depend largely on your response to them—in other words, you have to adapt.

Here are a few examples. Let's say you want a particular job, but it goes to the boss's nephew instead. Maybe you're in love with someone and want to marry him or her, but for whatever reason it doesn't work out. Perhaps the company you work for goes out of business, and you lose your job. A loved one dies. You're injured in an auto accident or suffer a serious disease. The list of possible scenarios is endless.

These are the proverbial cards that you have been dealt. You can't trade them in for another hand; you must play the cards you have right now. Now is when you must adapt. Recognize the reality and respond accordingly.

George Washington is one of my favorite historical figures. Perhaps his greatest trait was his ability to see a situation as it really was, not as he wished it to be. His actions were guided largely by the situation itself: he planned his moves to make the best possible use of the circumstances, and wherever possible, he tried to turn those circumstances to his advantage.

You can do the same thing. It's a two-step process. First, view every situation through realistic eyes. Don't kid yourself. Second, shape your response to make the most of the circumstances.

Of course, this doesn't mean that you should give up your personal autonomy or allow yourself to be tossed and turned like a boat without a rudder. No sailor can control the wind, but a good sailor uses the existing wind to sail to the destination of his own choosing.

You have to expect things of yourself
before you can do them.

—Michael Jordan

Lesson 13:
Your expectations will usually come true.

It's called the Pygmalion Effect—also known as the self-fulfilling prophecy—and it's real. If we expect a positive outcome, we'll probably get it. If we expect a negative outcome, it's likely to happen.

A lot of research has been done on school children in this area. Robert Rosenthal and Lenoir Jacobson performed studies at elementary schools where teachers were given the names of a select group of high-achieving students. The teachers were told that because these kids were so intelligent, they would probably excel over their lower-performing classmates.

Sure enough, those smart kids performed like smart kids. They got good grades, and they generally showed significant improvement on end-of-the-year tests. There was only one catch: the "smart" kids weren't really any smarter than the others. In fact, they had been chosen completely at random.

The real difference had been the expectations of the teachers—and as a result, their treatment of the students. Later studies have confirmed this effect in adults as well.

Your expectations become your own self-fulfilling prophecy. This applies to events both big and small. The reason is simple: if you really believe that you will do a great job, your subconscious mind will guide your behavior to be consistent with that belief, and you will indeed be an outstanding employee, student, or whatever.

If, on the other hand, you view yourself as not being good at something, you'll have no motivation to improve. What would be the point? You know you can't do it, so why waste your time trying to get better?

Do you see where this is going? Just knowing about the self-fulfilling prophecy can be a tremendous help to you in your life. Remember: you have complete control over your own thinking. It naturally follows that you have control over your own expectations.

So what's it going to be? You can expect misfortune—and almost certainly bring it on—or you can expect great things from yourself. Just remember that you have no one but yourself to blame for your own expectations.

*Self-forgiveness means accepting the fact
that you will never have a better past.*

—Dan Sullivan

Lesson 14:
It's never too late.

You're lucky to have your whole life ahead of you. You're able to choose how you will live it. Many people wake up in middle age to the realization that the life they have lived is not the life they wanted. This often results in regret, disappointment, and a mid-life crisis.

I enjoy watching *Dog Whisperer with Cesar Millan* on the National Geographic Channel. It follows real-life dog expert Cesar Millan as he works with people and their pets. Millan finds that problem behavior is more often caused by the human owner than by the dog.

Many of his clients have rescued their pets from abusive or neglectful situations. The owners mistakenly believe that their dogs' behavior problems are caused by bad memories, when in fact the owner's worry is to blame.

Millan points out that dogs don't care about—or even remember—the past. "Dogs live in the now," Millan says. "They don't care about their past lives. If you give them exercise, discipline, and affection, they will be happy and well-adjusted."

Maybe we could learn a thing or two from dogs. Whatever bad stuff has happened in the past, leave it there—in the past. You're an adult now. Childhood was just the warm-up act; now is the time for you to take control of your own well-being. As Cesar Millan would say: live in the now. If a dog can do it, surely so can you!

Of course, you can't *just* live in the now. To paraphrase Dickens's *A Christmas Carol*, you should live in the past, the present, and the future. But don't let the past rule you.

Who you are today is a composite result of everything that you have experienced in the past. Recognize that fact, but resist the temptation to go back. Don't regret or wonder, "What if?" Your life is here and now. By the same token, you must look ahead, to the future. Decide where you want to go, and start moving in that direction. If you don't, you could find yourself in a life that goes nowhere.

So here's the trick: cherish all the good stuff from the past, let go of all the bad stuff, and envision the future that you want for yourself. Then use the present to begin creating that future.

Those who look for beauty, find it.

—Unknown

Lesson 15:
Relax, and expect the best.

Let's review the concepts we've talked about so far:

Your attitude is the prime factor in achieving long-term happiness, career success, fulfilling relationships, and triumph over adversity (Lesson 1). What's more, you have complete control over your own thinking (2). Thinking only of yourself is a recipe for disaster; personal fulfillment comes from improving the world around you (3). Happiness does not come from your circumstances—if it is to come, you must create it for yourself (4). And you *can* create it, here and now (5). Embracing personal responsibility gives you the ability to determine your own destiny (6). Your personal values system is the internal compass which guides your actions (7). Time is slipping by; you can't slow it down, so every moment is precious (8). Perhaps for the first time, you are now in a position to really live the Golden Rule (9). Forgiveness gives you the power to liberate yourself and others (10). The secret to living a regret-free life is to be bold (11). You can't always change your circumstances, but you can adapt and make the most of them (12). Your expectations will probably come true (13). Don't feel bad if you haven't made the most of your life up to now, because it's never too late to start creating your future (14).

The recurring theme throughout this list is as simple as it is meaningful: *You have the power to shape your own destiny.*

That is a fact. If you haven't thought about it before now, take a few minutes to let it sink in. That power rests entirely with you. Nobody can take it from you without your permission.

So relax and know that all is well. Start believing that life will bring you everything you want. Decide to take control of your destiny by taking control of your life. Expect the best, and know that it will happen for you.

part two

work
and career

Life is not divided into semesters. You don't get summers off, and very few employers are interested in helping you find yourself.

—Bill Gates

Lesson 16:
Life is different now.

Congratulations on your graduation. They call it a commencement ceremony for a reason: you're heading out on your own into the future. Life's great adventure is before you. If you embrace it, you can have a fuller, more meaningful life than you can possibly imagine.

Don't get me wrong. It won't be easy—nothing worthwhile ever is. And it won't be at all like the life you're used to. Life in the adult world is radically different from school life. For example, if you just graduated from high school, you're used to a life regulated by the school year and the school day. The school day is spent in a school building with others of about your same age. You change classes every hour or so. School ends sometime around 3:00 in the afternoon. The day closes with extracurricular activities and/or homework, and maybe a part-time job. College is different, of course, with its own routines and schedules.

Your authority figures are your parents, teachers and professors. Your parents provide money for the basics of life, as well as some luxuries. Adults are authority figures simply because they are adults.

But that life is over. As comfortable as it may have been, it was a child's life. You're an adult now. The life of an adult is better than that of a child—if you make it so. On the other hand, the responsibilities are much greater, and the price of messing up is much, much higher.

For one thing, instead of your parents providing for you, you'll have to provide for yourself. In our society, you're expected to pull your own weight. If you don't, you end up completely depending on others. So I expect you'll do what is necessary to make your own way.

The daily routine of an adult is generally determined by your job. There's no telling what your typical day will be like, but it is highly likely that your workday will be longer than a typical school day. And those frequent vacations and days off you're used to? In your first year on a job, you'll be lucky to get a week's vacation and a few holidays. Other than that, they'll expect to see you at work every weekday.

All of this is not to scare or depress you. Remember, an adult's life can be wonderful. But the change is sudden. Just try not to be too shocked when it hits you all at once.

*The be-all and end-all of life should not be
to get rich, but to enrich the world.*

—B.C. Forbes

Lesson 17:
Make yourself useful.

Having a good heart does not make you a good person.

That may sound callous, but think about it. What makes for a good person? Don't you think that a good person is one who makes the world better for his having lived there? The fact that you care about something means absolutely nothing to anyone other than you—until that care takes the form of *action*.

Let's carry the concept a step further. A caring heart unaccompanied by action is a recipe for unhappiness. Why? Simple. If you truly care, then you know you should be doing something, but because you're not, you feel like a failure—or worse, a fake.

Let's take a simple example. My Kiwanis Club spends a few Saturday mornings each year picking up litter along a local highway. One such day, as I prepared to leave for litter duty, I asked a friend if he wanted to come along. He said in all seriousness, "No, thanks. I think that's just for show, so other people will think you care. For me, it's enough to know I care—it doesn't matter if anybody else knows."

Hmmm. That's not an uncommon view for a kid, but it doesn't wash for an adult—even a young adult like you.

The truth is I didn't really care much about that road litter; I never really noticed it. And I doubt that anyone recognized my hunched figure as I picked up beer cans and McDonald's bags. But I was out there cleaning up while my friend was at home on the couch, "caring." Even though I didn't care very much, my actions made the world just a bit cleaner. Who felt better about himself afterward?

This big ol' world couldn't care less about your personal happiness—or about the fact that you "care." The world wants to know: what are you doing for *me*?

The first thing you should do when you get a job is get busy and try to make things a little easier on everyone around you. By doing so you'll quickly become a valuable employee, you'll put yourself in position for raises and promotions, and you'll feel good about the fact that you're making a contribution. Keep applying this simple concept, and you'll never be without a job for long.

Action expresses priorities.

—Mahatma Gandhi

Lesson 18:
Set your priorities, and follow them.

Earlier, we talked about living by a set of values. Priorities are driven by your values, and in fact some of your values may also double as priorities. But whereas your values are principles to live by, priorities are more like a set of rules. Think of your priorities as a list of the most important things in your life, in ranked order.

For many people, the basic personal priorities include family, career, and religious development, but personal priorities can go well beyond these. Some may set their leisure activities as a priority. Athletes place a high priority on improving their performance, musicians on practicing their craft. Young couples often want to save money for a new home or a child's education.

We need priorities because we have a limited amount of time. We want to make sure we spend our time on things that are important to us, rather than wasting time on worthless activities. Priorities are our way of budgeting our time so that we get to the important stuff.

Now that you've graduated, your priorities will become even more important. As we've already seen, time becomes more precious as you get older. And as you enter the world of full-time work, you're likely to find that your non-work hours are very valuable to you. You want to make sure you spend them on activities that are important.

You may have never thought much about your priorities, but they're there, all right. They reveal themselves in your behavior. Wherever you spend your time and effort, you'll find a priority.

Whenever our actions don't match up with our stated priorities, discontent is sure to result. A man may say that his children are his number one priority, but if he neglects them, then something's wrong. He either needs to change his actions or admit that his kids really aren't as important to him as he says they are.

Ask yourself: Where have I been spending my time? What are the priorities that are revealed in my actions? Are they the priorities that I want for myself? If not, now is the perfect time to set your priorities, and then reflect them in your actions.

Call on God, but row away from the rocks.

—Hunter S. Thompson

Lesson 19:
Use your God-given talents.

Broadcaster Earl Nightingale told the story of a clergyman who was traveling through a rural countryside when he came upon an extraordinarily productive and scenic farm. There were bounteous crops in neat rows, and all around the freshly painted farmhouse and outbuildings were flower beds and neatly trimmed shrubs.

The clergyman noticed the farmer taking a break from his work, so he took the opportunity to strike up a conversation. "The Lord certainly has blessed you with a beautiful farm," the minister commented.

"Yessir, he has," replied the farmer, wiping the sweat from his brow. "And I'm grateful. But you should have seen the place when he had it all to himself."

Many people just show up to work and do the bare minimum. They complete the tasks that are given to them—and that's about it. They never take the initiative to improve their workplace or to really serve the people around them.

Others see unexplored possibilities in even the lowliest of duties. They envision a well-tended farm where others see just a job. They throw themselves enthusiastically into every task, and as a result, they make everyone around them better.

You've been given a lot. You have a fine mind and at least a basic education. You have judgment and maturity, both of which will increase with time. And you live in a country filled with good people and limitless opportunities. So what do you plan to do with all these blessings?

If you believe in God, you may agree with me that he gives us the tools with which to make our own way and to make the world a better place. I don't pretend to know the mind of God, but I suspect he has given us all these tools so that we can use them to make reasoned decisions, to take decisive actions, and to work toward the advancement of those worthwhile values and priorities we set for ourselves.

Use those God-given talents. Apply them to your work, and it will sing.

Education's purpose is to replace an
empty mind with an open one.

—Malcolm Forbes

Lesson 20:
Knowledge has its limitations.

Studies have shown that there is almost no correlation between how smart a person is and how successful they become. Superior intelligence—even combined with education and knowledge—just isn't enough to make you successful. You need wisdom to go along with it.

I recently read about a young boy in India, Akrit Jaswal, who had an IQ greater than that of Einstein. In 2001, when he was seven years old, he performed a real-life surgical operation—I kid you not.

His eight-year-old patient had been so severely burned that her fingers had fused together. Living in a poor village, her family couldn't afford a real doctor, so Akrit was called in. The operation was a success, and before long Akrit became India's youngest university student. He showed a great gift for medicine. At age fourteen, he became convinced that if someone would fund a laboratory for him, he would be able to cure cancer within a year.

He traveled to London's Imperial College, where he met with some of the world's leading cancer researchers. He amazed everyone with the depth and breadth of his medical knowledge. But the researchers soon realized that, despite his obvious gifts, his theories were unworkable. He came away understanding that—as smart as he was and as much as he had learned—he had a very long way to go.

The end of this story has yet to be written. Akrit Jaswal may yet cure cancer, but I suspect it will take many years—and he certainly won't do it on his brainpower and knowledge alone.

Believe it or not, you're sorely lacking in the knowledge department. Do you have any idea how rudimentary a high school education, and even a degree from a very fine college, is? As necessary as such an education is, it's still just a start. Even scholars with doctorates often say that the biggest thing they have learned from their years of in-depth study is how little they actually know about their specialty.

Understanding the limitations of your present knowledge is one of the first steps down the long road to wisdom. The good news is that you already possess everything you need to succeed. Keep learning. The more you learn, the faster you'll advance in your life and career.

Life is half spent before we know what it is.

—George Herbert

Lesson 21:
Never underestimate the value of experience.

Young adults usually don't fully appreciate the value of age and experience. This frequently comes up during your first job search. The thought often goes something like this:

"They say they want someone with experience, but how can I get experience unless they hire me? And besides, my youth and energy more than make up for my lack of experience."

Well, the truth is that experience is the best teacher you will ever have. And while youth and energy are wonderful (as you get older, you'll envy those traits in younger people), experience is just as wonderful—and over time becomes even better. While youth and energy fade with time, your bank of experience continues to increase until the day you die.

We place a high value on those things that cost us a lot, right? Youth and energy are free; they are naturally present in young adults. But experience—ah, now *that* is earned. Experience is what Harry Truman referred to as "the school of hard knocks." Its cost is measured in time, sweat, and pain—the pain of your own mistakes. Abigail Van Buren once said, "If we could sell our experiences for what they cost us, we'd all be millionaires."

In his autobiography, *Up Till Now*, William Shatner describes how he learned to act, not by attending acting school, but by performing in plays. As a young member of a Canadian theater troupe, he played a variety of roles in a variety of shows in front of a variety of audiences. "I had no formal acting training," he writes. "I had my own method: I said my lines as if I were the character.... The audience taught me how to act. If I did something and the audience responded, I did it again. So this experience of working every night...was my acting class."

Think of the very best teacher or professor you ever had. Think of all the wondrous and important things you learned from her or him. All those lessons will pale in comparison to what you will learn from that greatest of all teachers: experience. You may not believe that right now, but I guarantee that you will one day. Class has just started.

Reread this page in twenty years, and see if you agree with me then.

I slept and dreamed that life was joy.
I awoke and saw that life was service.
I acted, and behold, service was joy.

—Rabindranath Tagore

Lesson 22:
Serve others, and you will be rewarded.

We talked earlier about making yourself useful. Here's another way to put it: serve others.

In his audio program *Lead the Field*, Earl Nightingale makes the point that the extent of your success will be in direct proportion to the extent of your service to others. Think about this for a moment, and you'll see that it makes perfect sense.

If an organization had an employee who did nothing—just sat around playing Solitaire all day—that employee wouldn't last very long. He or she would be dead weight. On the other hand, an employee who accomplished twice as much as the average worker would be considered indispensable, and would likely receive a higher paycheck and faster promotions than the average.

Employees will sometimes say, "They can't expect me to do that extra work," or "That's not in my contract." Then they complain that they're not paid enough or are not appreciated. But they're getting just what they deserve; to expect more is to deny reality.

It's a pretty simple concept: you can't expect something for nothing. You wouldn't expect to be hired to manage a large corporation straight out of school; you've done nothing to earn it. By the same token, you can't expect a big raise or promotion without making a sufficient contribution to deserve such a reward.

While all human beings have equal value as persons, some clearly have skills, training, and experience that are more valuable than others. One doesn't make it into this group right away; it usually takes years of concentrated effort to get there. These valuable people are in great demand precisely because they are so rare. As a result, they usually command higher financial rewards for their work.

But money is by no means the only reward to be had from work—indeed, it's probably less important than the personal fulfillment derived from a job well done. A fat paycheck is a hollow reward if it isn't accompanied by a sense of accomplishment and the satisfaction that you are making the world better through your work. So embrace the idea of service. That's where the real rewards are.

What you leave behind is not what is engraved in stone monuments, but what is woven into the lives of others.

—Pericles

Lesson 23:
Helping others is the only true wealth.

The world should be a better place for your having been here. That's the real point of life. And where better to serve others than in your chosen profession?

The pursuit of money is all well and good. But if it only served to enrich you personally, what good would it be? More to the point, what good would you be?

I once met a very wealthy elderly lady who gave me a tour of her palatial home. It was filled with many exquisite objects, including original pieces by famous artists. As I complimented her on all the beautiful things, she replied sincerely, "They are lovely, aren't they? After all, I think the only real point of life is to collect as many beautiful things as possible."

What a tragedy. Here was a woman with the means to do a great deal of good with her wealth, yet she didn't even realize it. Ebenezer Scrooge had nothing on her.

Contrast that conversation with the story of Mother Teresa. Born in Macedonia, a small country in southeastern Europe, she became a nun at the age of eighteen. For over

61 years, she worked in the slums of Calcutta, India, caring for some of the poorest, most neglected people on the planet. In 1950 she started the Missionaries of Charity, an order that serves the poorest of the poor throughout the world. She received the Nobel Peace Prize in 1979. Today, her order and its supporting groups—over one million coworkers worldwide—serve poor and outcast people across the globe.

When she died, penniless, in 1997 at the age of eighty-seven, Mother Teresa was in many ways the richest person on Earth.

Sure, it's great to have money. As Sophie Tucker said, "I've been rich, and I've been poor. Believe me, honey, rich is better." Just remember that there is more than one kind of wealth. If you ever have to choose—and you might—I highly recommend the non-money kind.

*It is in your moments of decision
that your destiny is shaped.*

—Anthony Robbins

Lesson 24:
Make a decision.

Want to know a secret? The very act of deciding is often more important than the decision you make. Here's what I mean:

In your life, you'll be faced with many decisions. Some will be important, weighty choices; some will be small and relatively inconsequential. In some cases, the right answer will present itself, so the decision will be easy. At other times, there will be no clear-cut "right" answer. You'll struggle. Which should you choose: door number one or door number two?

Here's my advice: decide. Pick one—either one. Make a decision—and then make the decision work.

Remember, this is a case where there's no clear-cut answer. Unless you're expecting additional information that will help you make a more informed choice, you'll just have to choose. So *choose*. Then, make a commitment to the decision you have just made, and make it *work*.

If there's no obviously right way to go, then there's probably no wrong answer either. In that case, either decision can work for you if you make up your mind to make it work. What you do after the decision is very important—probably more important than the decision itself.

Decision-making is an important skill for everybody, but those who are especially good at it are likely to go far in life. Here's another secret: the real skill here is decisiveness, which is the ability to *make* a decision—any decision—and follow through with it. Nobody can read the future. Just make that decision and start moving. Others will follow.

Now, of course once you start going down the road, if you find that you're clearly headed for disaster, then you may need to change direction. But even in that case, you have to start down the road before you can learn that it's the wrong road.

In Robert Frost's *The Road Not Taken*, the poet finds himself in the woods, facing a choice of two divergent roads. He must choose. Which road should he take? He writes, "[I] looked down one as far as I could/ To where it bent in the undergrowth." At crunch time, you can only see so far. The important thing is to choose a path and start walking.

Nobody who ever gave his best regretted it.

—George Halas

Lesson 25:
Commit to excellence.

My first job out of college was with a consumer finance company. This company loaned small sums to people so they could buy things like appliances, TVs, and stereo systems. Most of our customers didn't have much money—that was why they needed a loan to buy a television set—and many of them frequently fell behind in their payments.

My job was to phone customers who fell behind and badger them to send in a check. If they fell too far behind, I would have to go to their home—often with a U-Haul truck and police officer in tow—and repossess their furniture.

Not surprisingly, I hated that job. The hours were long and the work disagreeable. I spent my days phoning people who didn't want to talk to me—I had to use an assumed name just to prevent them from hanging up on me. When I finally did get someone on the phone, the resulting conversation was usually depressing. My success rate in collecting back payments was abysmal. Most of my coworkers were grouchy because none of them wanted to be there either.

Fed up, one day I called my father to share my misery and tell him that I was planning to quit. His response surprised me. He discouraged me from quitting. In fact, he suggested that the problem was not with the job but with me. "If you leave now, you will have been defeated by the job," Dad said. "Stick with it a while longer. Learn to like it—get good at it. Then, if you want to quit, you'll walk out with your head high."

Properly chastened, I went in to the office the next day with a whole new approach. I said to myself, "I have to be here all day, so I might as well do the very best I can." I worked harder and came up with new ways to reach my customers. And it worked. Before long, my success rate was up, people took my calls, and many of my customers started paying their bills on time. I found myself actually enjoying my job. When I finally quit a few months later, I left feeling good about myself and confident about the challenges ahead.

Whatever you find yourself doing, resolve to give it your very best. You'll find that you're more effective, the work will seem easier, and people will recognize you as a cut above the ordinary. Before you know it, you'll be leaving the complainers and slackers behind—and you'll be on your way to bigger and better things.

It is necessary to the happiness of man that
he be mentally faithful to himself.

—Thomas Paine

Lesson 26:
Live a life of integrity.

As we have said, personal happiness involves a decision, but along with the decision must come action— action that aligns your behavior with your values and beliefs. That's integrity.

In constructing a building, all the structural components must fit together perfectly for the structure to hold up against the forces of nature. When the pieces are all properly connected to one another, from the bottom of the foundation to the top of the roof, the building is said to have structural integrity.

The same holds true for people. Earlier, we talked about your values as well as your priorities. Your values and your priorities must be in agreement with each other, and your actions must be consistent with both. If you value honesty, you must tell the truth—all the time. If your family is important to you, you must spend time with them. If you prize friendship, you must be a good friend to others.

Every time your actions conflict with your beliefs, your own structural integrity is weakened. You'll have a problem any time that happens, and if the disconnect is major, you'll have a major problem.

A good example would be a public figure, such as a government official or prominent minister who rails against child abuse or pornography. If the official or minister gets caught doing the very thing he condemns, the result is justifiable public outrage. But even if the person doesn't get caught, he still has a huge problem. Imagine the self-inflicted torture of such a person. It would literally be a personal hell.

Obviously, this would be an extreme case and—one would hope—extremely rare. But none of us is perfect. To expect perfection from yourself is unrealistic, although it is a worthy goal. Everyone falls short of being their ideal person at some point and to some extent. The point is to make an honest effort to be your best self by consciously aligning your actions with your values and priorities. When you get off track, get back on.

Integrity is a crucial ingredient of a happy existence. As you strive to live each day with integrity, you'll view yourself as someone deserving of your own respect. You'll almost certainly like yourself.

What we call luck is the inner man externalized.
We make things happen to us.

—Roberston Davies

Lesson 27:
Make your own luck.

Luck is real. But hoping for good luck to come to you is a poor strategy. And using bad luck as an excuse to underachieve is just as weak.

Yes, you could win the lottery. People do all the time. Somebody has to win, as they say, so it might as well be you, right? All true—you certainly *could* win—but you won't. It's been said that the government-sponsored lottery is a tax on fools, and that's not far wrong.

Bad luck exists as well, but it doesn't have to rule your life. In 1876, a candy maker with a fourth-grade education opened a business in Philadelphia; it failed miserably. He moved to Denver, where he failed again. This was followed by more failed ventures in Chicago, New Orleans, and New York. Talk about bad luck.

Finally, after ten years and repeated failures, he returned to his family home in rural Pennsylvania, disgraced and broke. With one more loan, he started yet another candy company. Using everything he had learned from his string of bad luck, he was at last able to pull off a success—a big success.

The candy maker's name was Milton Hershey, and the successful company he started was the Hershey Chocolate Corporation. As of this writing, the Hershey Company has annual sales of almost $5 billion and the company itself is valued at nearly $12 billion.

It's been said that luck is what happens when preparation meets opportunity. That was certainly the case with Milton Hershey. At each of his "bad-luck" stops, he learned something that that would become useful one day. All of his experience and hard-earned knowledge contributed to his development of the formula for Hershey's Milk Chocolate.

If there is a secret to having good luck, it can probably be summed up in this famous quote from Samuel Goldwyn: "The harder I work, the luckier I get."

You can make your own luck as well. Step one is to take responsibility for your own success or failure. Do what you love, and stick with it. When you suffer a setback, take away useful knowledge from the experience. Have faith, and keep at it. You'll get lucky soon enough.

*I'll take fifty percent efficiency to get
one hundred percent loyalty.*

—Samuel Goldwyn

Lesson 28:
Loyalty, properly placed, will take you far.

Milton Hershey's rags-to-riches saga is more than the
story of just one man. Throughout his difficult journey to
success, the milk chocolate mogul had the undying support
of three people: his mother, his Aunt Mattie, and his friend
William Lebkicher. They provided Milton encouragement
and financial support. Had it not been for them, Hershey
would not have been able to succeed. And when Milton
succeeded, his supporters shared in the success.

That's loyalty. Loyalty has been defined as devotion to a
cause; we can also view it as devotion to a person. Sometimes,
the cause and the person are one and the same.

Loyalty is an important trait to possess, but you must
place it properly. Be sure that the person or cause to whom
you are loyal deserves your loyalty.

The Jonestown tragedy is a classic case of misplaced
loyalty. Jim Jones was the charismatic leader of a
religious sect. In 1978, he led his followers in a mass
suicide ritual where they drank Kool-Aid laced with
poison. Over 900 people died, including 276 children.
Jones certainly was unworthy of loyalty, and yet

hundreds were willing to go to their deaths for him—and take their innocent children with them.

By contrast, Milton Hershey used his wealth to build an entire town, complete with schools, housing for employees, public transit, and 150 acres of parklands. He also established a residential school for orphaned boys, to which he gave the vast majority of his wealth. The school is still in operation today, serving nearly 1,400 underprivileged boys and girls from across the nation. Clearly, Hershey was a man deserving of loyalty.

Employers prize loyalty in their employees. Loyal workers are partners in success: everyone is pulling for the enterprise to succeed. It's as if everyone were in the same boat, rowing together to get to the destination. A few people pulling in the wrong direction can wreak havoc.

When you find someone who truly deserves your loyalty, give it to them. If they're really worthy, they'll be loyal to you as well, and you'll both benefit.

If you're gonna be a bear, be a grizzly.

—Unknown

Lesson 29:
Put your shoulder into it.

Effort is essential to success, but it never ceases to amaze me how few people seem to understand that simple fact.

I have hired quite a few employees in my time; I have also fired a few. The old saying is true: it's hard to find good help. A good, hard-working employee is hard to come by. All it takes is a little honest effort and a good attitude to stand out.

Most employers have an awful time finding and keeping good employees. It seems that many people work harder at avoiding effort than they would at just doing a good job. They're determined not to do any more than the bare minimum. What's more, they think they are owed a living.

What these poor souls don't realize is that the world doesn't owe them anything at all. They seem to think that they can—and should—get something for nothing, or get more out of something than they put in. But that's not the way life works. Nothing worthwhile is accomplished without sacrifice.

Everything in nature operates in this way. Just spend a little time watching common tree squirrels on a fall day, and you'll see what I'm talking about. A squirrel must store sufficient food in order to survive through the winter. Have you ever seen a squirrel sitting, resting, and watching other squirrels gather nuts for him? Of course not. Every one of them works incessantly, collecting and storing his or her own food supply.

The same applies to people. It's natural for each of us to do our fair share, and a person who does less is bound to have a negative self-image. That person is like a leech, sucking from the efforts of others.

You would do well to let that sink in: *the world owes you nothing.* You must earn your keep, pull your own weight. One of the simple secrets to success is that if you pull more than your own weight—if you do more than you're paid for—you will stand out from the crowd. You'll automatically make yourself indispensable. And you'll almost certainly be rewarded for it.

Nothing is easy to the unwilling.

—Thomas Fuller

Lesson 30:
Enthusiasm is infectious.

It's true: nothing is easy to the unwilling. In fact, one might say that nothing worthwhile is ever easy. Life ain't for sissies, as they say.

But why would you want to make it any harder than it has to be? Why not do everything possible to make it easier and more enjoyable? Life is a great, fun adventure—and if you treat it that way, you'll lighten the burden for yourself and those around you.

Take the late Steve Irwin, Australia's famed "Crocodile Hunter," as an example. He was so enthusiastic about his work that you couldn't help becoming interested yourself. Irwin knew the secret value of enthusiasm.

There's no denying that people are drawn to enthusiasm. It's true that some people are enthusiastic to the point of being annoying, but that's not the person I'm talking about. I'm talking about the person who gets excited about doing worthwhile tasks, who throws herself into every assignment with energy and a smile on her face.

We've all known enthusiastic people, and we often wonder how they do it. Each of us has things that excite our own enthusiasm, but those are usually subjects or areas that hold a special interest for us. How can some people seem to be interested in almost everything?

The answer is simple: they *decide* to be interested, and in doing so, they decide to be enthusiastic. Enthusiastic people not only do a better job, but they inspire those around them to do better as well. Enthusiasm is a self-chosen trait that makes work easier and makes you more valuable to others.

Obviously, you'll find it easier to be enthusiastic about some jobs and subjects than others. And some days it will be hard to work up enthusiasm for anything. Do it anyway—it's worth the effort.

Don't fall into the trap of thinking that enthusiasm is for suck-ups. That's a juvenile attitude that only hurts you. You're not a juvenile anymore, and you can't afford to think like one. Enthusiasm can make your life easier, more fun, and more rewarding—both financially and otherwise. And as a bonus, your enthusiasm will also benefit everyone around you. Try it—you'll like it!

Without goals, and plans to reach them, you are
like a ship that has set sail with no destination.

—Fitzhugh Dodson

Lesson 31:
Set goals.

You're lucky to be reading this, actually. You're about to learn about one of the great secrets to success: goals. Although goals are vital to success, most people never give them a thought. So let's take a moment to think about them.

You set goals every day, whether you realize it or not. In its simplest form, a goal is just a decision to do something. "I'm going to get out of bed, take a shower, have breakfast, and go to work."

There—you've just set four goals. In no more than a couple of hours, you will have accomplished them all. And while you're carrying them out, you're setting new goals. "I think I'll stop and get gas. And when I get to work, I need to finish that thing I didn't get to yesterday." And so it goes, every hour of every day.

Now let's just carry that same concept a little farther— maybe a lot farther. The kind of goals we're talking about now are conscious, measurable, long-term goals.

When you were a full-time student, you probably saw little need for those long-term goals. As a kid, your goals were pretty much set for you by your parents, teachers, and school routine: get through the school year with good grades, have a fun summer, and go back to school the next year with the same goals. The process was so universal, simple, and repetitive that you likely gave it no thought at all.

The days of having your goals set by others are gone for good. From now on, you must set your own goals—and you need to start thinking much, much bigger than you have up to now.

Think of it as if you were taking a road trip. First, you decide where you want to go—your destination. Then you look at the various routes available and decide which one to take.

The destination is the goal. The route is your strategy for achieving the goal. It doesn't matter what the destination is or how far away it is; once you have settled on the destination—the goal—you know you'll eventually arrive. The actions you take between now and then will determine your success in getting there.

Decide now to be a goal setter. Your future depends on it.

Anyone without a sense of humor is
at the mercy of everyone else.

—William Rotsler

Lesson 32:
Never stop playing.

It hardly needs to be said that human beings would rather have fun than suffer through endless hours of drudgery and sorrow. The way you go through life—enjoying it, detesting it, or anything in between—is mostly a matter of attitude. And we've clearly established that you have the capacity to choose your attitude.

Still don't believe that? Consider the story of the Pike Place Fish Market in downtown Seattle, Washington. You may have had a job or two that you considered to be unglamorous—flipping burgers, mowing lawns, waiting tables, bagging groceries—but try being a fishmonger.

At Pike Place Fish Market, the workers get up at four in the morning and make their way down to the fish dock to meet the commercial fishing boats as they arrive with their catch. They prepare the cold, smelly fish and arrange them for display in the market—which, although covered, is open to the air. They open at 6:00 am and sell raw fish to various customers.

The work is hard and the conditions are often tough because of the cold, damp weather in the Pacific Northwest.

When the long day is over, the workers are tired, cold, and sore, and they stink to high heaven. You'd expect that most of them hate their jobs, and you wouldn't blame them if they did.

But the employees of Pike Place Fish love their jobs—and far from spending their workdays in drudgery, they literally have a blast from beginning to end. They joke with customers, throw fish at each other as if they were footballs, and laugh at themselves and each other from morning to night. The market is a beehive of activity and laughter; people come from all over the world to visit Pike Place Fish Market.

This little company has gained fame because its employees enjoy working at jobs that most people would hate. Their secret? In 1986, owner John Yokoyama and his team made a decision to have fun and to be great with people—and they've been doing it ever since. That fun is infectious: it rubs off on customers, who return it back to the workers. It becomes a self-sustaining cycle.

You're never too old to have fun—and whatever job you have, it can be fun if you choose to make it so.

*Give this to Clemenza. I want reliable people,
people who won't get carried away.*

—Vito Corleone

The Godfather by Mario Puzo

Lesson 33:
Be dependable.

Woody Allen once said that 90 percent of life is just showing up. It's sad but true: dependable people are hard to come by. The upside of that statement is this: if you are dependable, you'll always be in demand.

I was lucky enough to learn this secret after my junior year in high school. As the school year waned and it came time to find a summer job, my buddy Pat and I decided that we didn't want regular fast-food-joint or grocery-store jobs—we wanted to be our own bosses. So we started a lawn-mowing business with the grand name of A and P Turf Specialists.

We typed up some fliers with our name and phone number as well as a description of our services—grass cutting—and some prices. We stuffed about three hundred of them in mailboxes throughout local neighborhoods (the fact that this was a violation of federal postal laws was lost on us). And before we knew it, we had about thirty regular customers.

That summer and the next, Pat and I made much more money in fewer working hours than any of our friends. We quickly came to understand that the secret to our success was very simple: our customers could rely on us. Once a lawn got on our weekly schedule, we showed up every week without fail and mowed the grass. It didn't matter if it was sunny and sweltering or pouring rain—we showed up and mowed the grass.

We didn't deliberately set out to be dependable—teenagers seldom think that responsibly—we just knew we had a good thing going and didn't want to mess it up. And we needed the money.

This principle extends far beyond mowing lawns. If you do something that needs to be done—and do it reliably—you'll never go hungry. I met a high school student recently who has a trash collection business that puts A and P Turf Specialists to shame. This kid, with just the help of his grandfather, makes more money part-time than most adults ever make in their full-time jobs. And of course his secret to success is to provide a needed service that people can depend on.

If you're dependable, you'll find that people respect you, jobs will be easy to get and keep, promotions will come quickly, and you'll feel good about yourself and the contributions you make.

Me and Woodrow have always liked to get where we started for, even if it don't make a damn bit of sense.

—Gus McCrae

Lonesome Dove by Larry McMurtry

Lesson 34:
Finish what you start.

I enjoy playing golf, but I'm a poor golfer. My swing is somewhat shortened (a charitable friend has dubbed it "compact"), leading to short drives and frequent slices.

As you might imagine, I have received lots of detailed advice from friends and golfing partners on how to improve my game, but the best lesson I ever had consisted of a single word. After observing one of my truncated swings and the resulting truncated shot with its telltale rightward curve, my friend Marshall demonstrated a swing of his own and said simply, "Finish."

I knew instinctively what he meant. Dropping another ball from my pocket, I hit another shot. But this time, instead of my usual compact swing, I allowed the club's momentum to carry through the point of impact, all the way up past my shoulders, and over and around my head. The resulting shot, while not Tigeresque by a long stretch, traveled longer and straighter than I had any right to expect.

Most of the important lessons in life are very simple, and this one is a perfect example: Finish what you start. How many times have you heard someone say, for example, "I should write a book"? Yet, how many people do you know who actually have written a book, and seen it through to publication? Not many, I'll bet. Here's the way these things work: lots of people vaguely plan to do it, a few people start doing it, and a very few of those who start ever complete the project.

They say every good story has a beginning, a middle, and an end. The journey starts with a single step, but that first step is just the beginning. Real fulfillment comes after you have taken the *final* step, knowing that you have accomplished the goal you set for yourself. That knowledge gives you the confidence that you have what it takes to complete whatever you set your mind to. The next project won't seem quite so daunting.

And there's another benefit. Sad to say, but there are too many people in this world who, for whatever reason, don't finish what they start. Those who do are in the minority, and they enjoy a competitive advantage that only grows over time.

A real failure does not need an excuse. It is an end in itself.
—Gertrude Stein

Lesson 35:
Know when to fold 'em.

Have you ever known anyone who just couldn't seem to complete anything? This person may have great ideas, make great plans, and even get started on their plans. But they never seem to complete what they start.

If you're reading this book in order, you just read the bit about finishing what you start. But now let's look at it from the other side. If seeing a thing through to its end is the path to success, quitting before you're done is the definition of failure.

That's a harsh statement, I know. Oh, we could be nice and talk about the exceptions. But if we look at it honestly, there aren't that many exceptions. And being honest with yourself is an absolute necessity if you are going to be successful in life.

Besides, it's not as bad as it sounds. Failing at something is not the end of the world. Sometimes it makes sense to give it up and move on to something else.

I know a young lady who earned an undergraduate degree in business administration, then subsequently spent two years in the business world before realizing that she didn't belong there: she didn't enjoy it and wasn't any good at it. By quitting, she admitted to herself and the rest of the world that she was a failure at business. She then applied to medical school—it may sound strange, but it's true—and graduated at the top of her class. She is now a highly successful surgeon. What's more, she loves her work.

And there are countless other examples: Edgar Allan Poe flunked out of West Point. As a boy, John F. Kennedy failed to make the football team. A young Cary Grant was kicked out of prep school.

None of these success stories would have been possible without failure. Each of these people failed at something, and then turned to other pursuits before achieving greatness.

As we return to the hypothetical person in the first paragraph above, we see the difference between real failure and real success. The failure never follows anything through and therefore never really knows whether he could even be a success. He just makes excuses.

Kill the snake of doubt in your soul,
crush the worms of fear in your heart and
mountains will move out of your way.

—Kate Seredy

Lesson 36:
Don't be afraid to achieve.

This may sound strange, but some athletes actually appear to be afraid of winning. Such an athlete may have all the natural gifts and talents, but it seems that every time he's on the cusp of winning a big contest—a major golf tournament or an Olympic gold medal, for example—his talents inexplicably abandon him and victory slips through his fingers.

This same phenomenon often occurs among non-athletes. We've all known someone who has all the attributes of a high achiever but never realizes their potential. Don't let that happen to you. Psychologists will tell you that such problems may stem from an inner sense of unworthiness, but the topics we have covered in this section may have a bearing as well. So let's review.

Adult life is different from what you're used to, and the sooner you embrace it, the better (Lesson 16). Making yourself useful is the key to job security (17). Establishing priorities seems to smooth the way by keeping you aware of what's important to you (18).

You have many natural talents, but they're worthless if you don't use them (19). It's important to be smart and well educated, but brains aren't enough to make you succeed (20). In fact, experience may turn out to be the greatest teacher you'll ever have (21). If you focus on serving others, you'll eventually be rewarded for it (22). In fact, helping other human beings is itself the purest form of wealth (23).

One key to success is the ability to make a decision (24). If you commit yourself to excellence (25) and a life of integrity (26), you'll feel good about who you are and improve your chances of earning lasting success. Don't count on luck to see you through (27). Be loyal to the right people (28), work hard (29), be enthusiastic about what you do (30), and set goals for yourself (31), and luck will take care of itself.

Make your work fun (32). Be dependable (33), and finish what you start (34). Remember that failure can lead to success (35).

Don't be afraid to succeed. Keep telling yourself that you deserve it. If you apply all these lessons, you *will* deserve it.

part three

personal relationships

*Without friends no one would choose to
live, though he had all other goods.*

—Aristotle

Lesson 37:
Get off the couch and out into the world.

Life isn't lived alone. It's lived with others.

More often than not, elderly people will tell you they would much rather live at home alone than go into a nursing facility. However, when push comes to shove, it's often a different story.

My friend Alice was ninety-four years old when she had a serious fall in her home. She lay helpless on the dining room floor for almost two days before a visitor found her and called an ambulance. After a few weeks' recovery in the hospital, it was clear that Alice couldn't return home, so arrangements were made for her to enter an assisted living facility.

After a brief but difficult adjustment period, Alice came to love her new home. She gives many reasons for her contentment, but first among them is this: the company of other people. She doesn't attend the weekly Bingo games or sing-a-longs, or even participate in the frequent group shopping trips. She basically just sits in her private room all day reading, venturing out only to take brief walks and go for meals in the dining room.

So how does Alice interact with others? Several times a day, staff members stick their heads in her doorway to offer a snack or merely ask how she's doing. What's more, she has two other ladies with whom she takes all her meals. There is very little conversation at the table, but she wouldn't want to miss a meal with her friends. This simple human contact has made the difference between a merely tolerable existence and a life of joy and contentment.

If this is true of a ninety-four-year-old, how much more true must it be for you? Besides age, there's one important difference between Alice and you: while Alice has only to sit and wait for her social life to come to her, you have to get up and seek yours.

So get involved in life. Be active. If you find yourself spending more than a little time in front of the TV, you need more human interaction. Join a club or two, or three. Get involved in your church. Volunteer for worthwhile organizations in your community. Do things with friends.

We humans are social animals. A life lived in isolation is no life at all. Get up. Get out. Get going!

The only way to have a friend is to be one.

—Ralph Waldo Emerson

Lesson 38:
Be a friend.

How can you tell who your real friends are? Good question, and not always easy to answer.

A real friend is more than someone to hang out with. A friend is someone who will give of herself to help you, without any thought of what's in it for her. That's a pretty high standard, one that many people can't, or won't, meet.

But *you* must meet the standard. *You* must be a true friend to everyone you meet. *You* must be the one who is willing to lend a hand, to offer a warm smile, to ask—really ask—how the other person is doing, and then really want to hear the answer.

It's a simple thing, but one that many people never learn: you don't make friends; you earn them.

You may say, "That's all well and good, but what if I'm the one doing all the giving? Is the other person really my friend? Aren't they just taking advantage of me?"

Ah, there's the rub. It's the eternal chicken-and-egg question: Which comes first? You do. It's simple if you just think about it. You have complete control over your own actions, but none at all over the actions of others. So don't wait for the other person to do something for you; instead, look for every opportunity to do something for them.

Don't worry over whether your friends are taking advantage of you—don't even give it a thought. The reason to do good for others is because you want to—because it's the right thing to do—not in order to get some reward for yourself.

But the rewards will come, as surely as night follows day. For one thing, you'll have the satisfaction of knowing that you are being useful in the world, which is a wonderful reward in itself. And people will recognize your genuine care for them. Pretty soon you will have more friends than you can count.

It won't take long to discover who your true friends are. But keep on being a friend yourself—to everyone—and you'll have more than your share.

The family is one of nature's masterpieces.

—George Santayana

Lesson 39:
It's all about family.

A young child grows up worshipping his parents, believing they are the source of all knowledge. Comedian Jeff Foxworthy points out how easy it is for a parent to impress a toddler:

Child: "What's that, Daddy?"

Father: "Well, son, that would be a *cow*."

Child, awestruck: "Wooow!"

It doesn't take long for this mystic aura to wear off. By the time a child reaches the ripe age of fourteen, he often believes the equation has reversed: the parent knows virtually nothing while the kid has it all figured out. By the time he reaches his mid-twenties, however, the offspring begins to gain a realistic appreciation for his parents.

With young siblings, it's often a love-hate relationship. My brother and I swapped many a bruise during our childhood years, but each of us would have fought anyone who uttered an unkind word about the other. And, like many siblings, as we grow older, the "hate" fades while the love remains.

It's one of the fascinating truths of life that each person is distinctly unique, even from the members of his own family. Our differences are the source of plenty of strife, but in most cases, the family bond cannot be broken.

Every summer, my three siblings and I, along with all our spouses and children (about seventeen people in all), spend a week together in a large beach house. We live rather far apart and don't see much of each other during the rest of the year, so that week is a special time for us. But if you were a fly on the wall and looked around at everyone present, you wouldn't expect that this diverse group would choose to spend so much time together. We're all so different from one another. We don't seem to fit together—and yet we do, perfectly.

Such is the mystery of family, and the magic cannot be replicated by any other group. The family is the one place where everyone knows one another intimately—faults and all—and still chooses to accept one another unconditionally. You almost have no choice: You're all stuck with one another.

Your family can be a great source of strength, comfort, security, support, and joy. Do everything in your power to preserve it. Nothing can replace it.

The woods are lovely, dark, and deep.
But I have promises to keep,
And miles to go before I sleep,
And miles to go before I sleep.

—Robert Frost
"Stopping by Woods on a Snowy Evening"

Lesson 40:
Keep your promises.

In the classic poem by Robert Frost, a traveler finds himself pausing on a road during a snowfall. On one side of the road is a frozen-over lake, on the other a beautiful wooded area. Having witnessed many such scenes during my childhood in northern Michigan, I can testify to the awesome, silent beauty of the moment.

The writer is so enchanted and so weary from travel that he considers putting off the rest of his trip while he remains here, absorbed in the wonders of nature. This thought lasts only briefly, however, as he reminds himself, "I have promises to keep." And so he continues on his journey.

I have asked myself many times: What promises? What's so important that this guy can't stop few hours for some well-deserved rest? Maybe he's carrying Christmas gifts in his sleigh and doesn't want to disappoint his children. Perhaps he promised to help a friend with some important task. Or maybe he just told his wife he'd be home for dinner.

Actually, it doesn't really matter, does it? A promise is a promise, and it must be kept. That's the trouble with promises: they are easy to make but not always easy to keep. What's more, the bigger and more important the promise, the harder it is to carry out.

When you were a kid, you fooled yourself into thinking that it wasn't a promise unless you said the words, "I promise." You know better now. Whenever you tell someone you're going to do something, you've made a promise; you have to take it seriously. But surely some promises are more important than others. Do you have to keep them all?

One option is to just not make any promises; that way, you never have to worry about keeping them. Another option is to not take your promises seriously: keep the promises that are easy and blow off the ones that are hard. Neither of these choices is satisfactory because they're easy but irresponsible, leading inevitably to a poor reputation and low self-esteem. There's no way around it: you have to make promises, and you have to try to keep them.

Inevitably, there will be times when a promise must be broken. You can minimize those times by thinking twice before making a promise. But once a promise is made, it's out of your mouth—so take it seriously.

We shall never know all the good
that a simple smile can do.

—Mother Teresa

Lesson 41:
Smile, darn ya, smile.

The simple smile carries immense power. It's one of the greatest secrets to success—both in business and personal relations. Everyone possesses this secret tool; it costs nothing, requires almost no effort, and produces immensely positive effects almost every time it appears. Yet an astonishing number of people seldom make use of it.

Play along with me here. Smile—right now. Don't be embarrassed, nobody's watching. Smile a big smile—a smile that tightens your cheeks and wrinkles your eyes. How does it make you feel? Good, right?

That's not just you, it's science. Studies have shown that infants begin smiling when only days old; blind infants smile even though they have never seen a smile. Many research papers have documented the effects of smiling, and in almost every case, the person on the receiving end of a smile forms a positive impression of the smiler. A smiling person is seen as approachable and friendly.

When you smile at someone, it gives them the impression that you like them, which in turn makes them want to like you. At the very least, you let them know that you're happy to be there. You put the other person at ease.

That doesn't mean that you have to walk around all day with a goofy, artificial grin on your face. But just think about it for a moment. Consider a few people you know who seldom smile, and then think of some who smile a lot. Whom do you prefer to be around? Everyone would rather spend time with a cheerful person than a grouch.

You may have seen the *Saturday Night Live* sketches called "Debbie Downer," featuring Rachel Dratch. The scene always showed a cheerful group of family or friends. Debbie, dressed in drab brown, would inevitably ruin the fun with a depressing comment. As she looked directly into the camera, her frown was accompanied by the descending "waaah-waaah" of a muted trombone.

The sketch was so popular because we all know a few Debbie Downers. Nobody wants to spend time with them; they don't have many friends, and you cringe when you get a phone call from one. A smiling face—along with the avoidance of ill-timed negative comments—will assure that you don't become a Debbie Downer yourself.

*You think you're hot snot, but you're
really just cold boogers.*

—Playground insult

Lesson 42:
A little humility never hurt anybody.

Think back on your high school years. Who was the
most popular person in your school? We're not talking about
the captain of the football team or the head cheerleader
(although it might have been one of them). I'm thinking of
the one individual that everybody liked and respected, the
person you couldn't help but like because he or she was just
so darned nice.

Now think of another person from your present life.
Again, we're looking for the one person against whom it
would be virtually impossible to have any hard feelings,
a through-and-through good guy. Repeat this exercise
a few more times and you're likely to develop a lineup of
wonderful, special people in your mind's eye. What do they
all have in common? Yes, they're all nice, but what does
that mean, really?

I'd guess that each of these people is approachable,
friendly, industrious, helpful, generous, and pleasant to
talk with. And if you think about it, you'll probably agree
that this combination of qualities is usually accompanied
by a healthy dose of humility. These special people may

have good reason to think very highly of themselves and act accordingly—but they don't. Otherwise, there's a good chance you'd hate their guts. It's the humility that makes a person like that tolerable.

Now let's approach it from another direction. Think of someone who is arrogant and overbearing, who treats others as if they were beneath him or her. I would wager that, regardless of any positive qualities this person has, you may find it hard to like them. It is almost impossible to like someone who thinks they're better than you. In many cases, that high-and-mighty persona often covers up a secret insecurity.

The great Winston Churchill was an excellent example— with a twist. Despite numerous personal doubts, he really did think of himself as better than others, referring to himself as a "great man." Because of that, many people had a great personal dislike for him.

In others, insecurity may manifest itself in an excess of humility. The overly humble person is always bad-mouthing himself; nothing he does is ever good enough. This person, too, can be difficult to be around.

So what's the moral? Be humble, but give yourself your due. Know that you're every bit as good as anybody else— but no better.

*Apologize for your mistakes. It will help disarm
your opponents and reduce defensiveness.*

—Dale Carnegie

Lesson 43:
When you're wrong, apologize.

There's no way around it: many times in your life,
you will do or say something you shouldn't. It may occur
in a moment of thoughtlessness; it may be completely
unintentional. Worse, you may deliberately do or say
something you shouldn't. You're human, and you will
certainly mess up again and again. Every once in a while,
you'll mess up big.

Apologize. Do it immediately and sincerely. Don't delay,
and don't do it halfway ("I'm sorry if I caused any problems,"
or "I'm sorry, *but...*"). You must show that you know you've
done wrong and are truly sorry. It's hard—sometimes very
hard—but it beats the alternative every time.

Consider the sad case of Marion Jones. A world-class
sprinter, she won five medals at the Sydney Olympic Games
in 2000. She was accused of steroid use but vehemently
denied the accusations for several years. She even filed a
$25 million lawsuit against one of her accusers, claiming
that he was trying to ruin her reputation.

Unfortunately, the accusations were true. In 2007, Jones
pleaded guilty to lying to federal investigators. She was

disgraced, stripped of her Sydney medals, and sentenced to six months in prison.

Immediately after pleading guilty, Jones stepped out of the courthouse and made an emotional apology in front of news cameras. It made for a heart-wrenching sight: this smart, articulate, charming person stood before the nation and admitted, "I have betrayed your trust.... I want you to know that I have been dishonest. And you have a right to be angry with me.... I have let my country down."

She said all the right things. Unfortunately, many listeners found it impossible to believe that she was really sorry. After all, she had lied so many times before. Imagine how different it would have been had she come clean when the question first came up. She would still have been disgraced, but the public would have been more inclined to forgive her. As it was, she made it much harder on herself.

When you mess up, apologize at once; take responsibility before the situation gets out of hand. Apologize sincerely and completely. Admit to yourself and those you have hurt that you have done wrong and that you want to make it right. It won't be easy, but you'll go a long way toward healing the wound you have caused.

If one could only learn to appreciate the little things.... The little things are what life is all about. Search your soul and learn to appreciate.

—Shadi Souferian

Lesson 44:
Be an appreciative person.

Who are the important people in your life? Your parents? Friends? Brothers, sisters, or other family members? Boyfriend or girlfriend? How grateful are you to have them in your life? And how do you express that gratitude?

If you think about it for a minute, you have so much to be grateful for. All those important people in your life, for starters. But consider some of the other things that make life meaningful, interesting, and fun. Let's look at a few more.

In the people category, there may be coworkers, neighbors, business associates, customers, the lady at the convenience store who always has a smile. The kid who mows your lawn, the writer who produces an interesting column for your local paper, the mail lady, a friendly waitress, or even the highway patrolman who let you off with a warning.

Now let's look at the non-people category. Your pets, that old reliable car you drive, your favorite jeans, a club or church, your favorite chair, the perfection of a flower, fall colors, a blue sky. You get the picture.

The point here is to recognize that there are many, many things to be grateful for. See the wonders around you, both big and small. Feel appreciation for all those things every day. Develop what many have called the "attitude of gratitude."

That attitude of gratitude allows you to appreciate the wondrous world around you; it takes the focus away from "me" and places it outside yourself. Oprah Winfrey tells her fans, "Be thankful for what you have; you'll end up having more. If you concentrate on what you don't have, you'll never, ever have enough."

But don't stop at just feeling thankful. *Express* your gratitude. Say thank you to your waiter. Smile at people passing by. Tell your loved ones how much you care about them, and do something nice to prove it. Put your attitude into action. As William Arthur Ward once said, "Feeling gratitude and not expressing it is like wrapping a present and not giving it."

It's not true that nice guys finish last. Nice guys are winners before the game even starts.

—Addison Walker

Lesson 45:
Play nice.

Have you ever noticed how cynical college students can be?

I attended a small college where most students got to know the professors and administrators fairly well. Mr. Campbell, the vice president of finance, was a fixture on campus for decades and was especially well known for his friendliness. His signature greeting was, "Hi! How ya doin'? Good to see ya!" Regardless of the occasion, regardless of the person being greeted, the greeting was the same.

"Hi! How ya doin'? Good to see ya!"

Needless to say, many students made fun of Mr. Campbell behind his back. Upon his approach, they'd exchange knowing glances at the anticipated salutation. He never let them down. Students who didn't know him well assumed that he couldn't possibly be that nice; they assumed the greeting was a way for him to cover up the fact that he couldn't remember anybody's name.

How wrong they were. When Mr. Campbell died a few years ago, the outpouring of love and respect was overwhelming. It turned out that he did remember names—lots of them, generations of them. Stories poured in describing his generosity, his kindness, the sensitivity he and his wife had shown when students had needed substitute parents.

He really *had* been that nice. The greeting had real meaning. He had made a huge difference in the lives of many, many people.

Here's another little story. After earning an MBA, a young man returned to his hometown to take his place in the family business. He was young, energetic, and well educated, and he had little patience for the niceties of the office environment. "I'm not here to make friends," he told me once. "I'm here to do my job and be successful."

As you might expect, he soon alienated himself from most of the employees. They left him to sink or swim on his own—and for a while, he sank. Fortunately for everyone, he soon learned that he couldn't be successful without making friends. And that, my friend, is the point.

It takes very little effort to be nice. Yet the rewards—for you and everyone around you—are out of all proportion to the cost.

There are two things I hate: intolerance and the French.

—Unknown

Lesson 46:
Be tolerant.

Don't you love that quote? It humorously highlights an attitude that is common in so many people. We're very tolerant of the things and people we like; it is the stuff we don't like that irritates us. So in order to be more tolerant, we need to widen our view of what—and who—we like.

In order to really be tolerant of someone, you must first respect them. My favorite definition of respect comes from Annie Gottlieb: "Respect ... is appreciation of the separateness of the other person, of the ways he or she is unique." If you really appreciate those differences, then tolerance will naturally follow.

This type of tolerance can be directed toward an entire group of people (the French, for example) or can occur between individuals. Tolerance toward an entire class of people is often easier than tolerance toward an individual.

What if someone doesn't respect—or is not tolerant of—you? How should you react? With tolerance, of course. Your appreciation of another person's uniqueness should not be dependent on their appreciation of yours; that's a losing game that will lock you both in a downward spiral.

Somebody has to be the one to break the cycle, to be the first to show respect. That may be a bitter pill to swallow; it requires humbling yourself before someone who doesn't appear to respect you. You know that you will be the bigger person for giving in, so don't let stubbornness or vain pride keep you from doing what you know is right.

There's another type of tolerance, and it may be the toughest of all. I'm talking about the personal challenge of tolerating the insensitivities and hurtful comments of others. Even if you tell yourself that insults and verbal barbs shouldn't bother you, they do hurt.

Here's where your respect for others can be severely tested. When it happens, the best defense is a healthy sense of your own self-worth—tolerance of yourself, so to speak. Longfellow put it this way: "He that respects himself is safe from others. He wears a coat of mail that none can pierce."

So be tolerant of others—and of yourself.

Don't you trust me?

—Every teenager ever

Lesson 47:
There's a difference between trust and faith.

See if this sounds familiar. A teenager tells her parents that she's going to a party at a friend's house. The mother starts asking questions: Who is the friend? Where is the house? Who will be there? Will there be adult supervision? Will there be drinking? When will you be home?

At some point during this exchange, the inevitable teenager question arises: "Don't you trust me?" The mother replies that she does indeed trust her daughter. "Well then," comes the retort, "why are you asking so many questions?"

Regardless of where the conversation goes from here, what usually is *not* said is that while the mother may trust her offspring, she probably doesn't have an abundance of confidence in her ability to handle every situation that comes up.

That's the difference between trust and faith. In order to be a responsible adult, you must be deserving of both. Trust generally comes first. You earn it over time by being honest and upright, and by having a good heart and good intentions. Faith comes later, after you have faced a variety of adverse situations and proven that you can handle them responsibly.

Trust is essential, but it's not enough. You trust the waiter to handle your dinner order and credit card payment. But would you have enough faith in him to let him manage your entire life savings? Of course not. In order to have faith in someone, you need to know them well; you need to have seen how they act and react in a variety of difficult situations; you need to have faith not only in their honesty but also in their abilities. You need to know that you can count on them.

You may have occasionally heard someone talk about another person as their rock. That is an indication of complete faith in another, and it's the highest compliment one human being can bestow on another.

As you go through life, you would do well to remember this concept. It will come in handy both now—as you separate those persons in whom you can place faith from those whom you can merely trust—and later, as you work to earn the trust and faith of others. Later still (much later, we hope), you may want to keep all this in mind when you start having conversations with your own teenaged kids.

Laugh at yourself first, before anyone else can.

—Elsa Maxwell

Lesson 48:
Don't take yourself too seriously.

Confidence can show itself in interesting ways. One of the most interesting—and enjoyable—is the ability to laugh at yourself.

Psychologists tell us that, contrary to what you might expect, self-effacing humor actually indicates a high level of self-confidence. Someone who is able to laugh at himself is perceived as strong and likable. This is actually a double benefit: You're seen as having a good sense of humor as well as a healthy dose of humility. It makes you more approachable.

President Ronald Reagan was a master at this type of humor. Regardless of politics, he was universally admired for his ability to use humor to turn his perceived weaknesses into strengths while at the same time disarming his opponents.

Reagan was seventy years old at the beginning of his first term—the oldest elected president in history. While many considered his age a weakness, he made fun of it. "I have left orders to be awakened at any time in case of national emergency," he once said, "even if I'm in a cabinet meeting."

During a reelection campaign debate (when he was seventy-three), Reagan quipped, "I will not make age an issue in this campaign. I will not exploit, for political purposes, my opponent's youth and inexperience." His opponent, Walter Mondale, was fifty-six and had served two terms in the Senate and one as vice president, but the joke still worked.

Perhaps the best Reagan story came when he was rushed to the hospital after being shot in an assassination attempt. As he was wheeled into the operating room, his survival still in question, he looked around at all the surgeons and said, "I hope you're all Republicans."

Remember, we're talking humor here, not self-loathing or self-pitying comments. We all know people who are constantly putting themselves down in some way or another—and it's depressing rather than funny. But an occasional joke at your own expense can be just the thing to make everybody feel a little better.

Life is much too short to take anything too seriously—especially yourself. Lighten up. Laugh at yourself. It's a sign of strength, not weakness.

Be who you are and say what you feel, because those who mind don't matter, and those who matter don't mind.

—Dr. Seuss

Lesson 49:
Don't hold back; tell us how you really feel.

Be forthright in dealing with others. Just as you should always do what needs to be done, you should always say what needs to be said.

We've talked before about honesty, but forthrightness goes beyond honesty. Forthrightness is speaking out when it isn't easy—telling someone what they need to hear, even if it might hurt.

Some things are hard to say, but you should say them anyway. That's part of what it means to be a friend.

One big reason to be forthright is to avoid the phenomenon known as groupthink. Groupthink is the tendency of a group—work team, committee, family, or social group—to make poor decisions because nobody in the group is willing to speak up in opposition to a bad idea.

The *Challenger* Space Shuttle disaster is one well-known and tragic example of groupthink. Even though engineers recommended against launching the Challenger in the frigid temperatures of January, the committee responsible for the final decision brushed off the concerns, in the process sending seven astronauts to their deaths.

Young people in social settings often find themselves in groupthink situations—what your parents refer to as peer pressure. Parents worry that teenagers will make bad decisions about drinking, drugs, and sex because they aren't yet confident or secure enough to speak up against groupthink. As everyone knows, failure to speak up can have dire consequences for a kid.

The consequences don't get any less important as you progress through adulthood, but your capacity to speak up for yourself improves. Many times you will doubtless find yourself in a difficult position, where those around you are in agreement but you strongly disagree. You'll know that you should speak up, but you'll also know it will be risky. What will you do?

This can get tricky, because there may be a point beyond which you shouldn't carry your case. Where is that point, and how will you know when you get there? That's something you'll have to decide in each situation. One thing's for sure, though: you're always better off saying what you think. You can't count on anybody else to.

*The greatest weakness of most humans is their hesitancy
to tell others how much they love them while they're alive.*

—O. A. Batista

Lesson 50:
Love deeply and freely.

Love somebody. Love not just one somebody, but many.
Don't be afraid to give your love away, because it always
comes back to you.

There are many kinds of love, of course: romantic
love, parental love, family love, love for friends. In fact,
friendship in itself is a form of love. A healthy life requires
love. But for some reason, too many people don't fully allow
themselves to love.

True, you take a chance when you love another person.
You run the risk of caring more for them than they do for
you—I guess that may be one reason why so many people
tend to ration their love. But if you think about it, the risk
is minor compared to the reward. A caring relationship
provides joy, security, and strength to both parties.

I'm not suggesting that you have lots of romantic lovers,
of course. One at a time is plenty—and one for a lifetime
is best in this category. In the family department, you're
limited by the size of your family. But beyond that, there's
no limit on the number of caring relationships one person
may have. Each relationship opens the way for others.

It's not enough just to love; you must express your love. Love that's felt but not expressed is like a bouquet of roses left in a closet—the point is to share it. The ways you express your love depend on the nature of the relationship and can be verbal or non-verbal.

Verbal expressions: "When was the last time I told you how great I think you are?" "I really enjoy talking with you." "You're all right; I don't care what your mother says." "You make my day." "I'm so glad we're friends." "Our relationship means a lot to me." "I love you."

Nonverbal expressions: A hug. A kiss on the cheek. A warm handshake. A pat on the back. A playful push. A smile. Walking arm in arm.

When you express your love, you are communicating a simple message from one human being to another, a message that enriches both the giver and the receiver. It's been said that if we all had only five minutes left to live, the world's phone lines would be jammed with people trying to tell others they love them. Don't wait until it's too late; do it today, and every day.

Don't spend time beating on a wall,
hoping to transform it into a door.

—Dr. Laura Schlessinger

Lesson 51:
You can't make another person change.

You already know this, right? Let's review anyway.

"I know he drinks too much, and he doesn't pay attention to me. And he tends to be irresponsible. But I just know that once we get married, my love can change all that."

Don't kid yourself. If there's one thing we have clearly established by now, it is that each individual makes his or her own changes. We may want to change to please someone else, but we actually *do* it only to please ourselves.

Every high school and college has its share of on-again, off-again couples that are clearly not meant for each other, but for some reason keep getting back together. Anyone with any sense can see that they are incompatible, but each seems to live under the delusion that, with a little tweaking, their partner will be just perfect.

While this type of soap opera can be a source of some entertainment for observers, it's bad business for the participants. They fool themselves into thinking that everything will work out one day, but the fairy tale almost never has a happy ending.

When you're a young person in love, you desperately want the relationship to work out. What too many people never understand is that, unique as you are, there are many people out there with whom you can be happy. It doesn't make sense to stay in a rocky relationship, especially if the problems go beyond arguing and hurt feelings.

These are some examples: Someone who is abusive—either physically or emotionally—is extremely unlikely to stop, no matter how much remorse they feel after an incident. A cheating boyfriend or girlfriend is likely to become a cheating spouse. Alcoholics can fight their way out of addiction, but only when they truly recognize their problem and take action themselves—they can't do it for someone else.

No one—*no one*—can fundamentally change just because another person wants them to. It is not humanly possible. If you find yourself in this situation, face the hard facts. Cut your losses and move on. Being alone is always preferable to being in a bad relationship. Anyone who doesn't understand that has a big problem of their own.

*The cost of success will be too high if you
choose not to lead a balanced life.*

—Linda Stryker

Lesson 52:
Balance in all things.

Despite what you may have heard, you can't have it all.

Stories of great success are often accompanied by terrible tragedy. That's what happens when something becomes so important that everything else takes a back seat.

In order to become very wealthy, a person usually has to devote all of his effort and energy to making that dream come true. Personal and family relationships often suffer as a result. The same is true with celebrities: the divorce rate among entertainers is extremely high.

The late Paul Newman was an exception to the rule. At his death, he had been married to the same woman, actress Joanne Woodward, for nearly fifty years. Although in great demand, Newman made a conscious decision to limit his acting schedule. That decision allowed him to pursue an interest in auto racing and start a food company, Newman's Own, which donated all of its profits to charity—well in excess of $200 million over the years. In addition, he was active in liberal political causes and campaigns. He did all this while maintaining an extremely successful acting and directing career as well as a healthy home life.

The rule of balance holds true in nearly every facet of life. A balanced diet is preferable to one that concentrates on a single food group. One glass of wine with dinner is good for you, but too much alcohol consumption results in all kinds of serious problems. Too much time in front of a television can rot your brain. Spend too much time at work, and your home life will suffer; don't spend enough, and you're likely to lose your job.

Life is a series of choices. Every time you say yes to one thing, you say no to something else. In fact, every time you say yes to something, you're saying no to a lot of things. When you accept a job offer, you're ruling out any other job possibility—at least for now. If you make the decision to be a full-time stay-at-home parent, any career plans are put on hold until you change your mind. When you say yes to a marriage proposal, you say no to every other potential spouse.

And here's something else you should know. People who live unbalanced lives are not very interesting. Balance is almost always in your best interest; keep that in mind every time you say yes.

All who would win joy, must share it;
happiness was born a twin.

—Lord Byron

Lesson 53:
Share.

As a child, you were told to share, and you did it because you had to. As a grown-up, you share because you want to. The rewards of sharing and giving are always greater than the rewards of receiving.

Sometimes, receiving is in itself a form of giving. When you know that someone is excited about giving you something, you want them to experience that joy. This often results in a comment such as, "Oh, a purple plaid polka-dot tie—just what I wanted!"

There are lots of ways to share; giving a gift is just one. Donating money to your favorite charity, church, or college annual fund are others. Sharing a meal with a friend is another. Paying someone a compliment is yet another.

By the way, you need to learn how to *take* a compliment if you don't know already. Here's the entire lesson: When someone compliments you, respond by saying, "Thank you." That's it. Don't pooh-pooh the compliment out of a sense of humility: "Well, thanks, but I really didn't do anything worth noticing. It was so-and-so who did most of it, and I only ..." Blah, blah, blah.

Enough, already! This person is trying to be nice to you, and by rejecting the compliment you're really rejecting their effort to be nice. By forcing them to defend their comment, you turn it into an argument. A compliment is as much for the benefit of the giver as the receiver. So share a little good feeling with someone who wants to share with you. Just say thank you and leave it at that.

One of my favorite things to share is time. You can do this by helping a friend move into a new apartment or mowing an elderly neighbor's lawn. Volunteering is a great form of sharing, and there are lots of organizations and projects deserving of your time. Help build a house for a poor family, serve meals at a homeless shelter, or tutor underprivileged kids. Try it, you'll like it.

It really is more blessed to give than to receive. You know you're an adult when you reach the point at which giving is more fun than receiving. And therein lies the sublime and ironic secret of sharing: the more you give—in gifts, money, kind words, and time—the richer you will be.

Variety is the spice of life.

—Unknown

Lesson 54:
Cherish diversity.

One of the many interesting aspects of the early teenage psyche is the desire to be—as much as possible—exactly like the other members of their peer group. At a time when the young person is just beginning to create her own unique identity, the overwhelming need is to fit in. This tendency shows up in everything from clothes to hairstyles to vocabulary.

In that environment, different is considered bad. In the eyes of a young teenager, anyone who is unique is an object of criticism and derision.

But as you have no doubt learned, different is not necessarily bad. In fact, diversity can be a great source of strength. You've certainly learned this if you've gone off to college. Perspectives broaden, opinions evolve, and stereotypes melt away as you meet new people and discover different ways of looking at things.

Everyone knows that America is a melting pot. Our nation is a unique blend of nationalities, ethnic groups, religions, languages, and cultures, all of which combine to create a unique and vibrant culture of our own. There are times when it's not pretty, when groups pit themselves against one another. But you'll probably agree that our country's diversity is one of its greatest strengths.

Okay, so how does this apply to you personally? As you go through life each day, diversity will be all around you, and it will show up in a variety of ways. You'll be bombarded with different personalities, opinions, attitudes, and points of view.

Resist the temptation to simply reject any of this. You'll never meet anyone who won't have something to teach you, if you just pay attention. They may change your point of view on a subject, challenge an assumption, or give you a new way to look at something. You'll certainly learn how another person acts, thinks, or looks at the world.

At the very least, you'll be entertained by the amazing patchwork of human existence surrounding you. Even better, you'll learn how to relate to—and get along with—a wide variety of people. And you might just get a little smarter in the process.

To have a good friend is one of the highest delights in life; to be a good friend is one of the noblest and most difficult undertakings.

—Anonymous

Lesson 55: Relationships matter.

Each human being exists within the context of other human beings, and the quality of our interactions largely determines the quality of our lives, so it's important to put some thought and effort into those relationships. Let's review:

First, don't expect the world to come to you. You have to take the initiative and get involved (Lesson 37). In order to have a friend, you must first be a friend yourself (38).

Value your family members and show them your love and appreciation (39). A promise is a promise, and you need to keep the ones you make (40). It takes very little effort to smile, and the rewards are out of all proportion to the costs (41).

Be humble, but not too humble (42). When you're wrong, don't make excuses. Apologize swiftly, emphatically, and sincerely (43). Feel and show appreciation for others, for what they accomplish, and for what they do for you (44).

It's simple, really. Be nice (45). Be tolerant by expanding your definition of what you like and by refusing to be hurt by the insensitivity of others (46). Be deserving of both trust and faith (47). Don't be afraid to laugh at yourself. Life is a lot more fun if you don't take yourself too seriously (48).

Be willing to say those things that need to be said, even when it's hard to do so (49). Life has little meaning without love, so love deeply and freely (50). Understand that trying to change another human being is a loser's game (51).

The world offers limitless opportunities, but you can't have it all. Some choices can have a tremendous effect—either positive or negative—on your relationships, so choose carefully and try to maintain balance in all things (52).

Great relationships are all about sharing—sharing of material possessions, money, time, kind words, and love (53). Finally, cherish the tremendous variety of people, personalities, religions, and cultures around you (54). By valuing diversity, you open up possibilities you never knew existed. And those possibilities can make young adulthood a beautiful, exciting, magnificent time of growth.

part four

facing adversity

*If we had no winter, the spring would not be
so pleasant: if we did not sometimes taste of
adversity, prosperity would not be so welcome.*

—Anne Bradstreet

Lesson 56:
Life is full of troubles,
and you can handle them.

Inevitably, you will have problems. Real problems. Serious problems. There will be struggles, disappointments, misunderstandings, setbacks, rejections, failures, and heartaches. Some you'll see coming and others will appear out of nowhere. Any way you look at it, you're in for a load of troubles.

You will have to face them down—every one of them—and it's not going to be easy. It's never easy facing pain, but you must. The questions are: What will you do? How will you react?

Bernie Siegel once said, "One cannot get through life without pain.... What we can do is choose how to use the pain life presents to us." There are two important words in that quote: *choose* and *use*. We've talked about choice many times in our discussions, and here it is again. When you remind yourself that you get to *choose* what to think and how to react, things get a little easier. You realize that you're not powerless.

The other important word is use. Not only do you choose how to react, you also choose how to use the pain. That's right: pain can be a motivator, something we use to lift ourselves out of despair and into action.

I know of no one who personifies that attitude better than Brook Waddle. Brook was a high school senior—an excellent student, cheerleader, and homecoming queen with a bright future—until a terrible car wreck left her a quadriplegic.

During a year and a half of intensive therapy and four surgeries, Brook used her own pain to prevail, right where she was. She provided moral support to other patients at Shepherd Clinic in Atlanta. After earning her high school diploma, she set her sights on college and a career as an adolescent psychologist.

Brook's problems aren't over, of course, and neither are yours—in fact, they're just starting. When they come, don't let them beat you down. Choose your attitude and keep moving forward. Remember that the sun will still rise the next day, and that time really is a great healer. Pain is an essential part of life. As Garrison Keillor noted, "It's a shallow life that doesn't give a person a few scars."

If you're going through hell, keep going.

—Winston Churchill

Lesson 57:
Never give up.

Wilma Rudolph was born in rural Tennessee in 1940. Her family was large—she was the twentieth of twenty-two children—and very poor. She was born prematurely and suffered a series of major childhood diseases, including polio which left her left leg weak and deformed. Her doctor told her that she would never walk again.

Despite the poor prognosis, the Rudolph family worked together to improve Wilma's chances. She eventually learned to walk with the aid of metal leg braces; at the age of twelve, she discarded them and began walking on her own. Determined to become an athlete, she joined the basketball team at her segregated school, but didn't play in a single game for three straight years.

When she finally did get in, she became a star. She earned a track scholarship to Tennessee State University, even though her high school had no track team. She won three gold medals in the 1960 Rome Olympics—the first woman ever to attain such a feat. It would have been natural for the young girl to give up, but she persisted and prevailed.

Have you ever known someone who had plenty of brains and talent, but never stuck with anything long enough to make a successful go of it? The world is full of such people. They never learn the secret of persistence, of continuing to work toward a goal.

In the old *Star Trek* television series, they had a transporter beam, a device that could transport a person instantly across the great void of space. In the real-life world of achieving goals, there is no transporter beam. You have to make the journey yourself, one step at a time. You'll get knocked off course, sure, but you must get up, set your eyes back on the destination, and get back on track.

This quote by Calvin Coolidge sums it up beautifully: "Nothing in the world can take the place of Persistence. Talent will not; nothing is more common than unsuccessful men with talent. Genius will not; unrewarded genius is almost a proverb. Education will not; the world is full of educated derelicts. Persistence and Determination alone are omnipotent. The slogan 'Press On' has solved and will always solve the problems of the human race."

Press on, my friend.

Try not. Do; or do not. There is no try.

—Yoda
Star Wars Episode V:
The Empire Strikes Back

Lesson 58:
Determination and persistence go hand-in-hand.

Determination is closely related to persistence. You can't really have one without the other.

You make up your mind that you will succeed at something, and that nothing will stop you. "That's the way it is," you say to yourself. "I will do this thing—and that's all there is to it." That's determination.

Then you set out to make your decision a reality, and it doesn't work. But you don't leave it at that. You get up, dust yourself off, and try again. You keep trying and keep trying until it works. That's persistence.

You may sometimes be able to succeed with just determination—if you succeed on your first attempt. But you must always be prepared to try, try again. Thomas Edison is the best example of determination I can think of, so let's look at a few of his quotes.

The creator of some of the most important inventions of all time, Edison recognized the necessity of both determination and persistence. "The first requisite for success," he said, "is the ability to apply your physical and mental energies to one problem incessantly without growing weary."

You've probably heard that Edison failed thousands of times in his efforts to create the first incandescent light bulb. As his vain attempts continued, he was ridiculed by the press and the public, but never allowed himself to be discouraged. "Results!" he said. "Why man, I have gotten a lot of results. I know several thousand things that don't work."

"Opportunity is missed by most people," he added, "because it is dressed in overalls and looks like work."

Edison described the need for determination and persistence in this simple, yet profoundly practical statement: "The three great essentials for achieving anything worthwhile are, first, hard work; second, stick-to-it-iveness; third, common sense."

You have common sense, don't you? Just work hard and keep at it, and you'll be fine.

The only completely consistent people are the dead.

—Aldous Huxley

Lesson 59:
Be consistent—at least sometimes.

Did you ever have a teacher whose tests didn't match what she taught in class? We've all been there: You apply yourself and learn what she teaches. But once you start taking the test, you say to yourself, "I don't recognize any of this stuff." That's a sickening feeling, isn't it?

Or how about this: You see a newspaper ad for a beautiful big-screen TV at an incredibly low price. You hurry to the store, only to be told by the salesman that either: (1) they just sold out of that model and won't be getting any more; or (2) yes, they do have a few in stock, but it's really a lousy TV. In both scenarios, the next bit is always the same: For just a little more, I can sell you a much better model. Here, let me show it to you....

One scenario describes a bad teacher, the other a classic bait-and-switch ploy. Both make you feel cheated, and both are the result of inconsistency.

If you act consistently, others will know what to expect from you, and that's important. Everyone respects a teacher whose tests match what she teaches, even if the tests are hard. You know where you stand and what you need to do. There's no moving target.

It's the same way with your own personal behavior. You earn respect by showing consistency in your actions and responses. This is one of the characteristics of a good leader: When the expectations are clear and consistent, the leader doesn't have to constantly give orders. Everyone knows what is expected, so they're able to do it without being told.

Not only does consistency let others know what to expect from you, it lets you know what to expect from yourself. That's important when you find yourself in a difficult situation: you have an established pattern of behavior that you can follow regardless of how bad things get.

Consistency is also an important aspect of personal integrity. Integrity is the result of matching your actions with your beliefs and values. Inconsistency in either your beliefs or your behavior causes a breakdown in your integrity.

Now, don't get carried away and become boring. There are times when it makes sense to be a little inconsistent, if only for the fun of it. Part of the joy of life is the unpredictability of it all. But in most areas of life, consistency is a must.

If you can keep your head when all about you
Are losing theirs and blaming you....
Yours is the Earth and everything that's in it,
And—which is more—you'll be a Man, my son!

—Rudyard Kipling

"If"

Lesson 60:
Be gracious in every situation.

Dictionary.com defines the word *gracious* as "pleasantly kind, benevolent, and courteous." You've heard the term used in many contexts: Gracious in victory. Gracious in defeat. A gracious hostess. A gracious God. Grace under pressure (as expressed in the quote by Kipling).

For the purpose of this discussion, let's focus on how being gracious can help you deal with adversity. We know that every life has its share of troubles. The way you conduct yourself during the difficult moments has a huge impact on how well you manage those troubles.

It's easy to get emotionally worked up in a crisis. Emotions run high. Sudden problems often lead to panic, anger, fear, and indecision. Keeping your head under such circumstances is essential to managing the situation effectively.

I once watched a Little League baseball coach get so frustrated by an umpire's strike-calling that he threw a world-class fit in front of the team bench. As his nine-year-old players and their parents looked on in astonishment, the coach shrieked, cursed, kicked sand, and demanded to fight the umpire right then and there. You can imagine how all this went over. The coach lost all respect and credibility with his players.

Scenes like this one are repeated all around the country at youth and high school athletic events. Referees are the focus of all kinds of abuse, especially when the calls and the score aren't going the home team's way. What is amazing is the degree to which these officials—who are virtually volunteers—are able to absorb the taunts and insults with an appearance of outward calm.

That's what you want to do. Keep cool under pressure. If you get pulled over for speeding, be calm and polite to the officer. Apologize for not paying closer attention. You still might get a ticket, but if you fly off the handle you'll certainly get one. If this guideline applies to something as minor as a traffic ticket, imagine how much more important it is in weighty matters. A cool head can take you far in life.

But how do you do it? How can you keep your emotions from running away with your common sense? Like anything else, it's a choice. Tell yourself that you can handle it. Force your head to rule your emotion. It's not always easy, but you can do it. Keep working at it; you'll get better over time.

The best index to a person's character is (a) how
he treats people who can't do him any good, and
(b) how he treats people who can't fight back.

—Abigail Van Buren

Lesson 61:
Character counts.

Golf is a unique sport in that you get to keep your own score. There are no referees and no official scorekeepers other than the participants themselves. It's easy to cheat, so golfers are fond of saying that golf "builds character."

But what is character, exactly? So much has been written about the subject that it's hard to pick a single definition. My favorite comes from J.C. Watts: "Everyone tries to define this thing called Character. It's not hard. Character is doing what's right when nobody's looking."

Character is important for two reasons. It determines your response to different situations. If you get used to doing the right thing, you will automatically do the right thing when the pressure is on. And consistently doing the right thing makes you feel good about the person you are. That feeling encourages you to continue to do the right thing, which in turn makes you feel even better about yourself; this pattern will continue in a self-supporting cycle.

If people think of you as a person of strong character but you know that you aren't, you'll develop this recurring, sick feeling in the pit of your stomach. That feeling is the result of knowing that you're not who you pretend to be; it's the penalty of weak character. You are a fraud.

Fortunately, people will eventually come to see you as a person of character. "Character is like a tree and reputation like a shadow," Abraham Lincoln said. "The shadow is what we think of it; the tree is the real thing."

Just as character occurs within oneself, its rewards and punishments are internal as well. Character settles into your mind and heart—and yes, the pit of your stomach—where it takes up residence and nourishes your soul.

So how do you develop character? The same way you develop every other important trait: you take control of your thinking and then make a conscious effort to change your actions. As Helen Douglas wrote, "Character isn't inherited. One builds it daily by the way one thinks and acts, thought by thought, action by action."

Work to develop your character. You'll be glad you did.

No legacy is so rich as honesty.

—William Shakespeare

Lesson 62:
Honesty really is the best policy.

I have many friends who are followers of the Mennonite faith. Mennonites are devout, peace-loving Christians, modest and unassuming in their manner of dress and their dealings with others.

One central tenet of Mennonite doctrine is the importance of telling the truth in all situations and to all people. No deceit, no evasiveness, no fibbing—even to spare another's feelings. To a Mennonite, there is no such thing as a "little white lie."

In fact, Mennonites do not swear oaths, even in a court of law. Why would they? Their faith requires them to be forthright and truthful at all times; swearing an oath implies that you might not tell the truth if it weren't for the oath.

Imagine living your entire life in this way—being 100 percent honest in every statement you make to every person you meet every single day. I know what you're thinking, and yes, that kind of truthfulness could get you into trouble. Most of us would rather say, "Well, Mabel, you're looking very nice today," even if we're thinking, "Mabel, I can't believe you wore that hideous dress again."

So let's grant ourselves the latitude to not hurt Mabel's feelings and talk about the bigger issue of honesty in our dealings with others. Why do people lie? Mostly for self-preservation, I'd say. You don't want to get in trouble or admit that you messed something up, so you lie about it and hope nobody will catch on.

But dishonesty is very difficult to maintain. One lie leads to another, and sooner or later you've constructed an entire house of cards that will come crashing down if one little piece gets disturbed. It's so much easier to tell the truth up front, pay the price of your actions, and increase your trustworthiness in the process. If you look back on your own experiences, you can probably remember times when you considered lying but ended up telling the truth—and were glad you did.

Sure, it's important for a kid to be honest. But for an adult, honesty is absolutely vital. A spotty pattern of deceit can make it impossible for you to even earn a living, while a consistent pattern of honesty will lead to a place of honor in the esteem of others.

One man with courage makes a majority.

—Andrew Jackson

Lesson 63:
Be courageous.

In my opinion, the phrase "go for it" is overused to a shameful degree. We tell a friend to go for it when encouraging them to get extra cheese on a pizza or to purchase a new suit. Trivial tasks shouldn't qualify as going for it because they don't involve significant success or failure; going for it should require courage.

Courage appears in many forms and in various situations, but the elements are always the same. Whenever you're confronted with a scary task, you need courage to overcome your fears and doubts. "Courage," as Mason Cooley wrote, "overrides self-doubt, but does not end it." You may be afraid, but you keep going despite the fear.

I have known many combat veterans, especially veterans of World War II. Every single one I have talked with readily admits to being terrified under fire. Despite the fear, they kept fighting because they didn't want to let their buddies down. The expression "shaking in their boots" was invented for these guys, but they soldiered on. That's courage.

Think of some events—big or small—in your own life that required courage. Asking someone on a first date, speaking before a group, applying for a job, skydiving, standing up for your beliefs in the face of opposition, taking the car keys from a friend who has had too much to drink. How did you feel? Scared, right? But the desire—perhaps the need—to do what needed to be done was stronger than the fear, so you fought through it. And most of the time—though perhaps not always—I expect that everything turned out as you had hoped.

As we have said elsewhere, nothing worthwhile is without cost. You may be afraid to do what it takes to get what you want: you might be embarrassed, you might get hurt, you might fail. That's where courage kicks in: yes, even though failure is a distinct possibility, you go for it anyway—because the potential reward is worth the risk. Now, that is really going for it.

Require courage of yourself. Call on it in tough times and when daring greatly. The more important the task and the greater the potential reward, the more courage you will need. Keep a supply of it handy. The more you have, the more successful you'll be in every aspect of your life.

Self-confidence is the first requisite to great undertakings.

—Samuel Johnson

Lesson 64:
Believe in yourself.

You can do virtually anything if you have confidence in yourself. If you don't have confidence, you must acquire it—otherwise, you'll be a failure before you've even begun.

Ever notice how some people have a talent that just seems to come naturally to them? Maybe it's music or basketball or trigonometry or cooking or public speaking. In many cases, the gift is as much a result of confidence as talent.

Michael Jordan didn't become the world's greatest basketball player through sheer talent; other players could dribble, shoot, and dunk as well as he could. His greatness stemmed from his belief that when the game was on the line and the final seconds were ticking off the clock, no one on the court could stop him.

As we have seen elsewhere, your expectations will usually come true. Michael believed in himself completely: he expected to win. And because he believed, he was successful. This is a self-renewing cycle that starts with confidence, which leads to success, which creates more confidence, and so on right up the ladder.

Confidence alone is not enough, of course. And that self-renewing cycle doesn't always work the way we wish it would. In fact, confidence in the face of failure can sometimes be the key to ultimate success. As Jordan himself once said, "I have missed more than 9,000 shots in my career. I have lost almost 300 games. On twenty-six occasions I have been entrusted to take the game winning shot...And I missed. And I have failed over and over and over again in my life. And that is precisely...why I succeed."

It has often been said that if you don't believe in yourself, you can't expect anyone else to either. That's absolutely true, so you must foster a strong belief in yourself. Make it a conscious conversation with yourself: "Whatever task is before me, I can handle it. I'm smart, I have a good education, and I'm learning more every day. The world is a better place because I am here, and I will do something to make it better this very day." You can do it. Believe it, and you will.

But what if you don't have confidence? How can you get it? Turn the page to find out.

Confidence can be developed by acting
as if you already have it.

—Brian Tracy

Lesson 65:
Act the part, and the rest will follow.

This may sound crazy, but if you act as if you're confident—even if you're not—real confidence probably won't be far behind. I know that sounds crazy, but it works. Let's consider it together, and I think you'll agree.

Think about your first day in high school. If you were like most freshmen, you felt nervous and more than a little intimidated. But you tried to act cool and confident—because the last thing you wanted was for other kids to see how scared you were.

But I'll bet that as time went on, your act became less of an act and more of a reality, until you reached a point where you were completely comfortable walking the halls. Virtually every high school kid goes through this process. You can probably think of other examples as well.

Not only does this concept make sense, it's completely natural. The more you do something, the better you get at it. The concept works with just about anything, which is why great athletes practice and great entertainers rehearse.

Some people appear to be naturally confident, but like anything else, confidence is developed over time. The more you do, the more you accomplish. And the more you accomplish, the more confident you become.

The great Dale Carnegie put it this way: "Inaction breeds doubt and fear. Action breeds confidence and courage. If you want to conquer fear, do not sit home and think about it. Go out and get busy."

Of course, anything can be taken too far. Try to be aware of the image you're creating. "We are what we pretend to be," Kurt Vonnegut once wrote, "so we must be careful what we pretend to be." I once knew a young assistant principal who tried to project an image of confidence, but it came off as arrogance to some people. As his pretend confidence evolved into genuine confidence, that negative impression faded.

The point is this: don't be afraid to step out of your comfort zone. Throughout your adult life, you'll need to do it again and again. That's what personal growth is all about.

Self-pity is our worst enemy and if we yield to it,
we can never do anything good in the world.

—Helen Keller

Lesson 66:
Feeling sorry for yourself is not a strategy.

If anyone ever had a right to feel sorry for herself, it was Helen Keller.

Born in rural Alabama in 1880, Helen lost both her sight and hearing when she was barely a year old. For the rest of her life, she had neither of the most basic senses that most of us take for granted.

The first few years of her life were, as you might expect, a blur of confusing smells, tastes, and touch sensations, none of which made any sense to her. It wasn't until age seven, when her family hired twenty-year-old Anne Sullivan to be her teacher, that the little girl's world began to come in to some kind of order.

Sullivan taught her young student how to communicate through sign language and later through speech. Obviously, nothing came easy to Helen, yet her life's achievements were remarkable. She earned a Bachelor of Arts degree with honors from Radcliffe College. She learned to read Greek, French, German, and Latin, and wrote twelve books of her own.

Helen Keller became world-famous as a speaker, author, and activist—all while living in a world with none of the technologies and tolerant attitudes we enjoy today.

So—would you like to tell the rest of the class what's holding you back?

Life's tough, and it can get worse. You sometimes get stuck with a lousy hand of cards. Bad stuff happens to good people, and vice versa. Nobody's going to give you anything. In short, life is not fair.

But it's your life, and it's the only one you've got. You can't wallow in self-pity, no matter how bad you have it. You've got to get up and do what needs to be done. What's more, no one is going to tell you what needs to be done—you're going to have to figure it out for yourself.

If you find yourself in a bad place, and you absolutely can't go on, go ahead and spend some time feeling sorry for yourself. But—forgive my harshness here—be quick about it. Take a few days. Then get up, dust yourself off, and move on. You can do it!

There are no secrets to success. It is the result of preparation, hard work, and learning from failure.

—Colin Powell

Lesson 67:
Over-prepare.

Few people can claim to have faced greater adversity than New York Mayor Rudy Giuliani did on September 11, 2001, as terrorist attacks sent two of our nation's largest and most important buildings tumbling to the ground.

Giuliani's management of the crisis and its extensive aftermath earned him universal praise and the nickname "America's Mayor." How could he have handled such an impossible situation so well? Preparation.

I once heard the mayor give a speech about the qualities of leadership. One of the keys he emphasized was preparation. He still points to the extensive preparations he and his staff had made for unforeseen disasters. Knowing that the island of Manhattan was vulnerable to a variety of serious crises—but not knowing what the specific situation might be—he made a variety of plans that might never be needed. As it turned out, those preparations were vital to the city's recovery.

Preparation is important in almost every area of your life, and it can make the difference between success and failure. It's not always fun to prepare, and it may take a lot of effort, but it's usually worth it. And you just might find a direct correlation between the amount of preparation and the success of your project.

Michael Jordan spent countless thousands of hours practicing alone before he began his superstar career. I suspect that he endured derogatory comments about his level of dedication both from other kids and adults. But something inside the young boy drove him on, ultimately resulting in his permanent place among the greatest athletes of all time.

Of course, MJ possessed a level of talent that most of us can only dream about, and I'm not suggesting that you should devote yourself exclusively to a single goal as he did. But neither should you neglect preparations that can boost your success and put you in a position to overcome some problem—or even avoid disaster.

The cases of Giuliani and Jordan, while very different, both emphasize the importance of preparation. In fact, you may sometimes need to over-prepare. It has been said that you can't possibly prepare for every possible situation—but you can prepare for 90 percent of them. If you do that, the other 10 percent will be much easier to deal with.

I think you should be an optimist. Optimists
have more fun than pessimists.

—Rudy Giuliani

Lesson 68:
Look on the bright side.

Optimism. Again, it is a choice you make. We keep coming back to the inescapable fact that you are in total control of your own life.

We've already mentioned that Rudolph Giuliani was the mayor of New York City during the September 11, 2001, attacks and their aftermath. He was faced with disaster on a scale most of us can only imagine. If anybody had a right to take a dim view of the world, it was Rudy.

And yet Rudy Giuliani was—and is—an optimist. Not only that, he tries to avoid negative people. In his speeches around the country, Giuliani often says, "I ran a lot of organizations. For the most part, the people I hired and promoted were the positive ones."

That should be enough to get your attention right there. If you want to succeed in the job market or business world, it is essential to have a positive outlook. Nobody wants a sourpuss working for them, or with them for that matter.

Think of someone you know who is always complaining, who never has a good thing to say about anyone, and when given a choice, assumes the worst is going to happen regardless of the situation. Is that person wildly successful? I doubt it.

The person you're thinking of probably doesn't have a lot of friends, either—nobody likes spending time with a grouch. Over the years, *Saturday Night Live* has had some memorable recurring sketches based on very funny pessimist characters, such as Ralph and Wendy Whiner and Debbie Downer.

We laugh at these sketches—just as we laugh at real-life whiners behind their backs—because gripers never seem to realize what a downbeat effect they have on those around them. But the opposite is also true: optimistic people have an uplifting effect on others. People are drawn to an optimist, because the optimist sees the best in everything and everyone.

Walk down any city street and pick out an optimist and a pessimist. They both live in the same world, yet the optimist sees it in a positive light and is generally happy, while the pessimist sees it in a negative light and is generally unhappy. This is a choice that each of us makes.

*It is better to suffer wrong than to do it, and happier
to be sometimes cheated than not to trust.*

—Samuel Johnson

Lesson 69:
Trust.

There's an age-old fable about a scorpion and a frog.
The scorpion wants to cross a river but can't swim, so he
asks the frog to give him a ride on his back. The frog at first
refuses, saying, "You'll sting me while I'm swimming, and
I'll die."

"That would be foolish," replies the scorpion. "If I were to
sting you, I'd drown, because I can't swim." This reasoning
makes sense to the frog, so he agrees. The scorpion climbs
aboard, and the frog starts swimming.

Halfway across the river, the scorpion stings the frog.
"Why did you sting me?" cries the frog incredulously. "Now
we'll both drown."

"I can't help it," says the scorpion. "It's my nature."

This simple story carries several lessons for us if we look
closely. One is that you can't expect someone to change his
or her nature. But there are also a couple of lessons having
to do with trust.

Can you trust everyone? Clearly not. But you can't
distrust everyone either. Life is built on human relationships,

and relationships are built on trust—trust that reaches out both ways. It starts with you: by being worthy of trust, you make it possible for others to trust you.

But then you have to extend trust to others. Some people never trust anyone; that course is both foolish and self-defeating. If you know in your heart that you're trustworthy, doesn't it make sense that others are as well? "Yes," you might say, "but *which* others?"

Ah, there's the rub, isn't it? Sometimes you can't know the answer to that question until after the fact. Like anything else, there is a balance here. "You may be deceived if you trust too much," Dr. Frank Crane once wrote, "but you will live in torment if you do not trust enough."

Frankly, I'd rather trust too much—and perhaps be burned occasionally—than not trust enough and live in fear that everyone is out to get me. The stakes probably won't be as high as those of the trusting frog in our story—and you may be surprised at how often your trust is rewarded.

There is no formula for success except perhaps an unconditional acceptance of life and what it brings.

—Arthur Rubenstein

Lesson 70:
Some things you just have to accept.

I once knew a man who accidentally ran over his own daughter in their driveway. The child was killed, and her father was the cause.

What a terrible thing to have to live with. The poor man and his wife suffered unspeakable pain, and his suffering must have been compounded immensely by guilt over his role in the tragedy. How could they possibly go on?

After years of painful reflection and soul-searching counseling sessions, they finally reached an inevitable conclusion: they simply had to accept what had happened and get on with their lives as best they could.

This is perhaps the most nightmarish scenario I can think of—a parent loses a precious, innocent child, and the parent is to blame. But even in this horrific circumstance, life goes on. Even here, the sufferer moves ahead with life.

What else could he do?

We've talked a lot about the influence you have over your own destiny, if you just take responsibility for your own life. It's true: your attitude and actions have the largest influence on the course of your life. But many things are beyond your control; you may get stuck with the consequences of events that you may not like.

Here's where your attitude—your mental toughness, if you prefer—comes in to play. You must accept what has happened and go forward with life, knowing that you cannot change the past; your only possible influence lies in the future.

This concept can be summed up in the words of the Serenity Prayer, commonly attributed to twentieth-century American theologian Reinhold Niebuhr: "God grant me the serenity to accept the things I cannot change; courage to change the things I can; and wisdom to know the difference."

Regardless of how bad today's troubles are, do you know what's going to happen tomorrow? The sun will come up, and life will go on.

Comfort and prosperity have never enriched the world as much as adversity has. Out of pain and problems have come the sweetest songs, and the most gripping stories.

—Billy Graham

Lesson 71:
Adversity really does build character.

Everyone faces problems in life—and some of them are major, life-altering events. When they come, you will somehow have to find the strength to face them down (Lesson 56). Let's review some character traits that prepare you for the tough times:

You'll need persistence, like Wilma Rudolph had (57). You'll need the kind of determination that allowed Thomas Edison to keep his head up through years of failure (58).

You'll need to practice consistency in your behavior, so that you'll know what to expect of yourself when challenged (59). Practice the art of grace under pressure so that you'll be able to keep a cool head when the pressure is on (60).

Practice doing the right thing—whether anyone's looking or not (61). Be honest, even when it's hard (62). Understand that there will be many times when you'll be afraid; believe that you will find the courage to face and overcome the fear (63).

Believe in yourself (64). Even if you don't have confidence, act as if you do; you may be surprised to find that real confidence will soon follow (65). No matter how bad things get, never give in to self-pity (66).

They say practice makes perfect. Go ahead and over-prepare; it can well mean the difference between failure and success (67).

Always try to look on the bright side. Optimism helps see you through hard times and is almost indispensable in achieving success (68).

In the midst of a cynical world, you must be willing to place trust in others, even when it requires a leap of faith (69).

Despite your best efforts, misfortune sometimes strikes. When it does, you may be able to do no better than to accept your fate and get on with your life (70).

Now let's discuss some commonsense tips for making your everyday life a little better.

part five

practical matters

Sometimes if you want to see a change for the better,
you have to take things into your own hands.

—Clint Eastwood

Lesson 72:
The human will is a powerful thing.

Did you hear the one about the guy who cut off his own arm with a dull pocket knife? It really happened, and the guy's name was Aron Ralston.

An experienced hiker and mountain climber, Ralston was hiking alone through a remote area of Utah canyons when a boulder shifted, pinning his right arm so tightly that he couldn't extricate it.

Ralston remained trapped against the boulder for five days before deciding that his only hope of survival was to cut off the arm with his multi-use pocket tool. So that's what he did.

After what must have been an incredibly painful self-amputation (during which he deliberately broke the two bones above his wrist and cut through the soft tissue with the dull blade of his knife), he rappelled down to level ground and hiked out of the wilderness to find help.

Ralston documented his experience in a book entitled *Between a Rock and a Hard Place*, published in 2004.

This is just one dramatic example of what a person can do when he or she is determined. Aron Ralston decided that he would not allow himself to die because of a 700-pound boulder that couldn't be moved, so he did the only thing he could.

One of the main themes of this book is the notion that you can do virtually anything you put your mind to. Now, let's consider that concept in bigger, more powerful terms. Much bigger. Much more powerful. Such as:

Stonehenge. The Great Pyramids. The Great Wall of China. The Taj Mahal. The discovery of the New World. The D-Day assault on Normandy. All of these great achievements were accomplished by ordinary people, not using twenty-first-century tools and technology, but with grit, determination, and the will to succeed.

What about you? What can you accomplish? Running a marathon? Sailing around the globe solo? Building a business empire? Expand your horizons. Believe in yourself. You have a huge future ahead of you—as long as you have the willpower to make it happen.

A disciplined conscience is a man's best friend. It may not be his most amiable, but it is his most faithful mentor.

—Austin Phelps

Lesson 73:
Discipline is no longer a dirty word.

When you were in school, you heard a lot about discipline in the classroom. You probably got sick and tired of hearing about discipline: Sit still. Be quiet. Single file. No gum. No running in the halls. The message that often came through was: no fun allowed.

In a way, Dictionary.com tends to support this impression. It defines *discipline* as "(a) Control obtained by enforcing compliance or order. (b) A systematic method to obtain obedience... (c) A state of order based on submission to rules and authority..."

But none of those is the *first* definition of the word; in fact, they are well down the list. Here's number one: Discipline is "training expected to produce a specific character or pattern of behavior, especially training that produces *moral or mental improvement* [italics added for emphasis]."

Ah, now that's more like it. Let's throw out all that classroom discipline stuff and start thinking of discipline as your friend. This type of discipline is not imposed by some authority figure bent on keeping you under control; it comes from within, and its purpose is to allow you to improve your mental and physical capabilities so that you can accomplish more and be happier. In short, the grown-up purpose of discipline is to help you live a better life.

Good things don't automatically happen if you just wait around long enough. We all know grown men and women who still live with their parents well into their thirties, waiting for a good job to come along so they can finally be out on their own. In many cases—certainly not all, but many—these folks simply have not imposed the self-discipline required to get where they want to be.

Continuing your education or training while working a full-time job requires discipline. So does getting up at 5:30 am to exercise. In order to advance in your job or career, you may have to arrive early or stay late, or find a way to get more done in the same amount of time as everyone else. In order to have a successful marriage or relationship, you must have the discipline to sacrifice some of your own personal desires for the sake of the other person.

All of these sacrifices will more than pay you back in a multitude of ways. Open your eyes and see discipline for what it is: your good friend.

The size of the future you actually experience will largely be determined by one factor: the people you choose to connect with.

—Dan Sullivan

Lesson 74:
Choose your friends carefully.

Your mother always told you not to run around with a bad crowd. That concept takes on added depth and importance as an adult.

In the professional world, people sometimes spend time networking: meeting and cultivating relationships with others in related professions or businesses. Networking is done at meetings or conferences, over lunch or dinner, or at social events. The idea is to build a network of friends that can help you along in your work and career. As they say, it's not *what* you know; it's *who* you know.

If networking sounds like a cynical process of making friends just so you can use them to get ahead, you're not the first person to reach that conclusion. And here's where it gets a little complicated.

At its crudest level, networking is indeed an exercise in "you scratch my back, and I'll scratch yours." But as many networkers have discovered, networking doesn't work at its crudest level. That's because real friendships are never based upon the selfish exchange of favors but upon genuine appreciation and affection for others.

A person who sets out to make "friends" just so they can be used for personal gain is likely to end up without any friends at all. People have an innate ability to recognize a false friend, and before long the poser finds himself on the outside looking in.

You already know that you have to be a friend in order to win a friend. If you greedily look upon friends as a source of favors, then you're not really a friend at all, so you're unlikely to get the favors you seek. But if you *don't* seek any favors, but instead demonstrate genuine care and support for others, then they'll recognize you as a friend—and the favors will come your way, because that's what friends do for friends.

Now turn the situation around. It is absolutely true that the right friends can be a source of great help and support, and the wrong friends can hold you back—not just in your work but in every aspect of life. You have the natural ability to discern the real friends from the posers. Don't maintain friendships with posers or negative people. Choose friends who are worthy of friendship, those who are genuine, positive, caring people. They will support your efforts to be your best and to achieve at the highest level. And they might even do you a favor or two along the way.

The simple act of paying attention can take you a long way.

—Keanu Reeves

Lesson 75:
Pay attention.

The more you shift focus from yourself to the world around you, the more you will be able to understand your place within that world. There is an exception, but let's start with the rule.

Have you ever known someone who seemed to stay in his or her own little world? They seem oblivious to everything that's going on around them. Some kids do this when they get immersed in a video game. My dad used to read the newspaper so intently that anything my mother asked him would be answered with an absent-minded "Umm-hmm...."

We all retreat into our personal worlds occasionally; surgeons do it while operating, authors do it while writing a book. There's nothing wrong with it. As the saying goes, "I'm in my own little world—everybody likes me there."

So spending a brief vacation in that little world every once in a while is probably healthy. But moving in permanently is not.

You need to pay attention to your surroundings, if only for your personal safety. Walking through a parking lot late at night can be dangerous if you're not paying attention.

Knowing what's going on around you at a wild party can keep you out of trouble, and perhaps out of danger. Being aware of the speed limit on the highway can prevent your getting a speeding ticket and help you avoid an accident.

Being aware can help in many other ways as well. At work, if you pay attention, you'll probably recognize needs that are not being met by anyone else; if you take up that slack, you're likely to be recognized as a go-getter. Paying attention to what you eat and drink can help keep you healthy and sober. Close observation of the people around you can help you determine who would make a good friend, who might not be trustworthy, and who can be counted on in a pinch.

Now here's the exception: Pay attention to yourself as well, without retreating into your own world. Determine what interests you, so you can learn more about it; perhaps this is the place for you to create a career. Be aware of when you're starting to get sick, so you can head off the illness early. Learn to trust your own instincts; they're usually right. Then use what you have learned about yourself and your surroundings to make a better place for yourself in the world.

A good listener is not only popular everywhere,
but after a while he gets to know something.

—Wilson Mizner

Lesson 76:
Shut up and listen.

Over the years, I have interviewed several World War
II veterans for the Library of Congress Veterans' History
Project. It's a simple procedure: you sit down with a veteran,
a microphone, and a video camera, and ask some open-
ended questions. The typical result is an astonishing flow of
stories and wisdom that's nothing short of inspirational.

These amazing men and women have, to a large extent,
kept their experiences to themselves for over sixty years.
They're now in their eighties and nineties, and they realize
that if they die with their stories untold, the world will be the
worse for it. So they're usually happy to have someone listen
and record the interview for posterity. And I can assure you
that the interviewer is deeply enriched by the experience.

Teenagers often complain that their parents don't
listen; employees complain that their bosses don't listen;
wives and husbands complain that their spouses don't
listen; teachers and professors complain that students
don't listen. Everybody's right, of course: we're all so self-
centered that we can't wait for everybody else to shut up so
we can talk.

But everybody values a good listener much more than a good talker. You've no doubt heard the comment, "He talks a good game." It's never a compliment. We all know people who talk too much, and most of us avoid them. Think about it—have you ever complained about someone who listens too much?

Listening is more than just waiting politely for the other person to finish. It involves paying attention, absorbing the message, and then reflecting it back to the speaker. You do this by nodding and making appropriately timed comments of your own. We're not talking about anything brilliant, just "Hmmm," or "I see," or the ever-popular "Mm-hmmm."

But good listening goes even further. You must be interested in the other person—don't just act interested, *be* interested. How, you ask? Just decide to. We've already established that you have complete control over your own conscious thoughts—so *decide* to be interested, and then listen accordingly. You'll probably learn something valuable.

God gave us two ears and one mouth; that proportion is just about right.

*Not everything that counts can be counted, and
not everything that can be counted counts.*

—Albert Einstein

Lesson 77:
Money is important.

You can't buy happiness, but you can rent financial security—and financial security can relieve a lot of stress.

Let's put money into perspective for a moment. You need it to pay the bills, put gas in your car and food on the table. Money also gives you choices.

With enough money, you can choose how to spend your time: Stay at home with your loved ones. Lie on a beach. Hike the Appalachian Trail. Volunteer for religious or community causes. Play golf. Climb Mount Everest. Write a book. Without the dough to make those choices, you're limited.

But it is also possible to be poor and happy at the same time. And many people of means are miserable despite their wealth.

There's a reason for this phenomenon, and it involves the importance that we assign to money. For some people, money is the most important thing in their lives. They become obsessed with living an affluent lifestyle. They must have the fanciest car, the biggest house in the most exclusive neighborhood, and all the other trappings of wealth. The pursuit and preservation of wealth becomes the central objective of their lives.

Have you ever known a teacher who was great at what she did and was clearly a happy person? Of course you have. The teaching profession is not known for its high salaries; in most states, it's hard to make a lot of money as a teacher. But you can make enough, and many teachers give up the opportunity to earn more money elsewhere because they love children and derive personal satisfaction from making a difference in the lives of kids. The same is true of countless men and women in many other vocations as well.

In fact, I have known several good and genuinely happy people who are quite poor. They work at menial jobs and struggle just to make ends meet every month, but they are content and seemingly carefree.

The bottom line here is that while money is a necessity, it's not a cure for unhappiness. Still, all things being equal, I'd rather be rich than poor, and I suspect you would, too.

If you would be wealthy, think of saving as well as getting.
—Benjamin Franklin

Lesson 78:
Save as much as you can, starting now.

This may seem a little premature, especially if you don't even have a real job yet, but one day you will want to retire. Who do you think will pay for that retirement? You will. And how will you pay for it? By saving—*now*—and not spending your savings until you do retire.

Let's take a look at what it means to retire. You stop working, yes, but your personal expenses continue. Some people actually spend more money in retirement than they did while working.

Why? Because they have more time on their hands. They're not tied up at work five days a week, and unless they sit at home, there's a good chance they'll find ways to spend money. Add to that the desire to take some vacations that had been put off while working, and you have a recipe for higher expenses in the golden years.

Now back to the cost of retirement. You need to start saving now—when you can least afford to—so that you'll have enough to retire when the time comes. Financial experts estimate that, with inflation factored in, today's young adult will need between two and three million dollars on their first day of retirement. That sounds like a lot, but it isn't—we're just talking about a modestly comfortable retirement.

Why is it important to start saving right away? Because the money you save today will be worth more than the money you save later. Here's what I mean:

Let's say you set aside $1,000 at age twenty-two. It earns 7 percent interest per year, compounded monthly. When you retire at, say, age sixty-five, that $1,000 will be worth about $20,000. By contrast, if you start to save the same $1,000 at forty-two, it will be worth less than $5,000 when you're sixty-five.

This little illustration shows the power of compounding: as your money grows, you earn interest not just on your original $1,000 but on the interest as well. It takes time for this to work the way it should—the more time, the better.

Get in the habit of saving now—and I mean right now. As mentioned earlier, you might think you can't afford to save right now, but you have to. Figure out a way to do it; you'll thank me when you're sixty-five.

Money can't buy happiness, but neither can poverty.

—Leo Rosten

Lesson 79:
There's a difference
between saving and investing.

Okay. Let's say you've decided that you need to start saving right away. What do you do with the money you save? You invest it. It's not hard to do, and you don't have to be rich to start. Exactly what is investing, and why would you invest money rather than just keep it in a bank?

In order to answer these questions, it helps to keep in mind that in money matters, as in all things, there is a balance—in the case of saving and investing, the balance is between risk and reward. If you want a higher return, you have to be willing to take more risk with your money. If you're unwilling to take risk, you must be willing to settle for a lower return.

Bank accounts have one great advantage and one potential drawback. The advantage is that bank deposits are insured by the Federal Deposit Insurance Corporation (FDIC), which is a United States government corporation. In other words, your bank accounts are guaranteed by the full faith and credit of the federal government. (There is a limit of $100,000 per depositor per bank.)

The disadvantage is that, because there's not much risk of loss, there's also very little reward. Generally, the rate of interest paid by FDIC-backed banks barely keeps pace with the rate of inflation, and sometimes it doesn't even do that. So if you want the spending power represented by your savings to increase, you'll need a higher rate of return.

That's where investing comes in. When you invest, you put your money at greater risk in the hope of earning a higher return. There's a spectrum of risk/reward options, from very low risk (where you must expect a very limited reward) to very high risk (where you can hope for a great reward but must be willing to lose your entire investment if it doesn't work out as planned).

For most people, a good way to start is to use a moderately risky, well-balanced mutual fund. Don't know what a mutual fund is? Then you'll need more information before you're ready to actually invest money. You may want to check out my book, *Low-Stress Investing* (available on Amazon.com). You can also visit investing websites. Some good ones are www.vanguard.com, www.fidelity.com, www.troweprice.com, and www.paxworld.com.

Never spend your money before you have it.

—Thomas Jefferson

Lesson 80:
Debt is bad. Really bad.

Debt is a really, really bad thing. It robs you of your future in order to buy stuff now. And the stuff you buy with borrowed money is purchased at a very inflated price, because you have to pay interest on it.

Want an example? Let's say you borrow $25,000 for a new car. The loan is for six years at 10% interest. Your payment is only $463.15 per month. Pretty good, huh?

Well, not really. In the first year, you will pay $2,356 in interest alone. By the time the six years is up, you will have paid a total of $8,347 in interest, raising the total cost of your car from $25,000 to $33,347.

What's worse, after the first year, you'll still owe about $21,800, but because most cars quickly depreciate in value, it'll probably be worth less than what you owe on it.

Debt can rapidly become a downward spiral. If you trade the car in after a few years but still owe more than the trade-in value, the dealer will add the balance to your new loan, and you'll be in even worse shape. And because the dealer may make more profit on financing than on the cars themselves, he is likely to focus just on the monthly payment, so it looks like a good deal on the surface.

As bad as this example is, credit card debt is worse—much worse. Interest rates on credit cards can be as high as 18% or more, and it's very easy—and tempting—to add more debt just by using your card.

Debt traps are all around, just waiting for you to step into them. Once you're in, it can be very painful to work your way out, and it could take years—maybe decades. In the meantime, the growing monthly payments can make it difficult for you to get by from week to week.

So how do you avoid the debt trap? Self-discipline and a little self-sacrifice. Save for big purchases. Buy a less-expensive car—preferably used. Use a debit card instead of a credit card; if you must use a credit card, pay it off each month. If you're planning to buy a house, make it a modest house, and save as large a down payment as you possibly can.

This is important. Stay out of the debt trap. Believe me: the less debt you have, the happier you'll be.

*Drive-in banks were established so most of the
cars today could see their real owners.*

—E. Joseph Cossman

Lesson 81:
A car is transportation, not self-expression.

Before we get too deep into this topic, let's look at why
we're talking about it in the first place. This lesson is all
about money and where you choose to spend it. You can buy
a car for $3,000 or for $100,000, or anywhere in between.
Essentially, they both accomplish the same thing: getting
you from Point A to Point B.

The reason I'm bringing this up is that young people—
and some not-so-young people as well—tend to spend a lot
of their money on a nice car. That's understandable; there's
something about the feeling you get from a new car. The
smell, the novelty—the newness of the entire experience is
exciting. Who wouldn't love to have a new car, especially if
you haven't had one before?

But life is all about choices. You can choose to spend
a lot on a new car, or you can choose to spend a little on a
not-so-new car, and save the difference.

"That's no fun," you may well protest, and I agree. But
if you've been reading the last few pages about money, you
know that getting caught in the debt trap is no fun either.
And while having the new car is a lot of fun for the first few

months, it doesn't take long for the debt trap to take away all the good feelings you had when you first drove off the lot.

To make this work, you have to think about it with your head rather than your heart. A good, safe used car that gets good gas mileage will be cheaper to buy and own than a new car. Go ahead and have the conversation with yourself. Tell yourself that the used car may require expensive repairs; go through the argument about not wanting to buy somebody else's problem; tell yourself that the new car will last longer, etc. Okay, done? You still know I'm right, don't you?

Let's be honest. I know that most people reading this will agree with everything it says, but will go ahead and buy the new car anyway. But unless you have a huge income that will allow you to save *and* make a big car payment at the same time, it will be a bad decision. And I guarantee that in a few years, you'll wish you had followed this advice.

The excitement of a new car is fleeting, but debt can hurt for a long, long time.

There is enough time for everything in the course of a day if you do but one thing at once; but there is not time enough in the year if you will do two things at a time.

—Philip Dormer Stanhope, Earl of Chesterfield

Lesson 82:
There's no such thing as multitasking.

A young man I know was in a job interview. He had applied to be an assistant principal at a middle school, a job that required a variety of tasks, some of which had to be done almost simultaneously.

"How many things can you do at once?" the interviewer asked. "Just one," replied the applicant. "But I can do it well." He got the job.

The truth is, you can do only one thing at a time. Just as the eye can focus on only one spot at a time, the human brain can concentrate on only one cognitive task during any given moment.

With modern technology, people seem to think that they can do several things at once: answer a phone call while sending an email and surfing the Internet, for example. It makes us feel more productive—almost superhuman.

But it's a myth. Research studies have shown that trying to do two things at once diminishes the quality of each task and actually reduces speed. But you don't need a research study to know that. If you've ever tried to do two things at once, you know that it doesn't work. It's not just you—nobody is superhuman.

Modern technology has enabled us to do several things in rapid succession. Years ago, when you wanted to call someone while you were in the car, you had to drive around until you found a phone booth—and hope you had a quarter. Today, you simply pick up your cell phone and make the call.

The problem is that if you're driving while talking on the phone, you're bound to be distracted. When it comes to causing traffic accidents, distracted driving is almost as dangerous as speeding or driving drunk. And it's not just cell phone usage that causes wrecks: turning to talk with passengers, operating a PDA, composing text messages, and fiddling with the navigation system all represent life-threatening forms of multitasking when combined with driving.

Take this advice: Don't try to do several things at once. Do one thing well—and quickly, if you have to—then go on to the next task. You'll get more done, do it better, and hopefully live to handle tomorrow's tasks as well.

*I cannot always control what goes on outside. But
I can always control what goes on inside.*

—Dr. Wayne Dyer

Lesson 83:
Keep control of yourself.

It always amazes me that so many people are willing to give up control of their own bodies and/or minds. Sometimes they give control to another person, and sometimes they give it to a substance or emotion.

Loss of self-control can take many forms, from bad to extremely bad. On the extreme end of the scale is the alcoholic. His life is controlled by the bottle; although he may tell himself that he can manage his drinking, it's really the drinking that manages him. The same is true for drug addicts or compulsive gamblers. These aren't bad people; they just have no control over their own behavior.

While addiction may be at the far end of the scale, loss of control on a smaller scale can be foolish at best and dangerous at worst. Want an example? I had a friend in college whose major form of recreation was getting as drunk as possible every weekend.

Joe was an excellent student—dean's list, pre-law, the whole bit—and he never drank during the week. But starting each Friday afternoon, he actually worked hard at getting drunk. And he stayed drunk all weekend. His antics at parties often proved to be an embarrassment to his fraternity brothers and whichever unfortunate young lady happened to be his date. He would say crude, hateful things, dance on the table in his boxer shorts, and—worst of all—get behind the wheel of his car and drive. One night at 3 am, he tripped in the parking lot of our dorm, and I took him to the emergency room to get his knee sewn up.

It's a miracle that Joe made it through college without seriously hurting himself or someone else. Fortunately, he eventually came to his senses, stopped drinking, and is now a respected attorney and family man.

Joe's story is neither extreme nor rare, and although he lost control frequently, it doesn't make sense to ever give up control. And there are so many ways it can happen: Getting drunk or high. Losing your temper. Making a decision based on emotion. Letting someone else talk you into something you're not sure about.

Personally, I hate the feeling of being out of control. It just doesn't make sense, and it can be dangerous. You know that you have complete power over your conscious thoughts and actions. Remember that, and always stay in control.

*I think you can accomplish anything if
you're willing to pay the price.*

—Vince Lombardi

Lesson 84:
You can't get something for nothing.

Nothing in life is free. You pay for everything you get—
and you *get paid* for everything you do, whether it is good
or bad.

Let's talk about the "pay for" part of that statement first.
The obvious example is buying things: when you purchase
a product, you pay for it with money. But this goes way,
way beyond spending money.

Virtually everything in life involves a trade-off. When
you say yes to one thing, you are saying no to something
else. Think about it for a moment, and you'll see the clear
truth in that statement. We've already established that
you can do only one thing at a time, so it naturally follows
that, whatever you are doing at any given time, there are
thousands of things you're *not* doing.

When you go off to college, you must leave your family
and most of your old friends behind, and put off starting
your career, at least for the time being. If you get married,
you commit yourself to one person exclusively, forsaking
all others. If your marriage doesn't work out—well then,

there's a steep price to pay for that as well. Think of any example you want, and you'll see that this rule applies.

Now let's consider the "get paid" part. This is also referred to as the cause-and-effect law of nature. Remember Sir Isaac Newton's Third Law: for every action, there is an equal and opposite reaction. This applies not just to physics but to all of life. You reap what you sow. Serve others, and you will be rewarded accordingly—the rewards may be financial or personal, and probably both. Live just for yourself, and you're asking for trouble.

You really can't get something for nothing. We've talked about it in several ways: To have a friend, you must be a friend. To be rewarded, you must first serve others. Nothing worthwhile is accomplished without sacrifice. It all boils down to this: the less you put into anything, the less you will get back from it; the more you put in, the more you'll get in return.

Earl Nightingale once used the analogy of a person sitting in front of an empty fireplace and expecting it to produce heat. You can't get heat until you supply the fireplace with wood and light the fire. As Nightingale would say, "Pile on the wood. The heat will come."

And the day came when the risk to remain tight in a
bud was more painful than the risk it took to blossom.

—Anais Nin

Lesson 85:
Act your age.

The last thirteen lessons have covered a variety of topics. Some involve universal concepts while others deal with mundane, everyday tasks. But they all share a single theme: living as a grownup in your everyday life.

Develop an appreciation for the immense, astonishing power of your own human will; with it, you can accomplish almost anything (Lesson 72). The concept of discipline, which is the bane of many a kid's existence, can now be one of your best friends—if you know how to use it (73). When it comes to human friends, choose them carefully. Posers and negative people constantly want to pull you down to their level, while true friends will help you to be your best (74).

Pay attention to what is happening around you; the simple act of awareness can benefit you in a wide range of situations and ways (75). One of the most important ways to pay attention is to listen—really listen—to others (76).

Like it or not, money is important—but only because of the security and choices it can provide. When money becomes an object in itself—when you fall in love with things and use money to define your own value relative to others—you're making a deal with the devil (77).

There will come a day when you'll need to have a very large pile of money saved up. The only way to get that pile is to save it rather than spend it. Start saving now; if you wait too long, the pile will never be big enough to meet your needs (78). When you do save, don't just put the money under the mattress or in a savings account; learn enough about investing to make your money work for you (79).

Debt is bad—the more debt you have, the worse off you'll be. It's very easy to slip into a hole of debt—and very hard to dig yourself out (80). One of the worst debt traps can be the purchase of a car, so set your vanity aside and buy a car that's safe, reliable, and cheap to own and maintain. You'll learn to love it (81).

Multitasking doesn't work—and can actually be hazardous to your health (82). Always try to keep in control. Losing control of your thoughts, emotions, or actions can lead to problems from which it can be tough to recover (83). Remember that you can't get something for nothing; there's a trade-off in every important decision you make (84).

As we said early on, life is different now. The old patterns of thinking and behaving just won't work anymore. Act like a grownup, and you'll be happy with the results.

part six

the inner you

Let the world know you as you are, not as you think you should be, because sooner or later, if you are posing, you will forget the pose, and then where are you?

—Fannie Brice

Lesson 86:
Be who you are, and be happy about it.

We've talked a lot about being honest with yourself, about understanding who you are. Let's take a moment to consider what it means to live each moment *at peace* with who you are.

Most of us know at least one person who is an authentic, genuinely nice person—someone who doesn't appear to have a deceitful bone in his or her body. You could also probably name someone who is the polar opposite of that first person, someone who, even if you like him or her, just seems to come off as artificial—a phony.

One of the great personal challenges each of us faces is being true to who we are while at the same time attempting to live each day as our very best self. The challenge involves trying to improve your attitude, skills, and contributions without pressing to the point of overreaching. Tim Russert was a good example of this type of person.

Born in 1950, Timothy J. Russert grew up in Buffalo, New York, in an Irish-Catholic, working-class family. His father, "Big Russ," worked for the sanitation department.

Tim attended a local Catholic school, received his bachelor's degree from John Carroll University, and earned his law degree from Cleveland State. In 1984, he joined NBC News, where he eventually became host of the Sunday morning interview show *Meet the Press* and chief of the Washington Bureau.

Russert's on-air personality was always warm and apparently genuine, although most viewers obviously didn't really know the man. But then he died suddenly on June 13, 2008, and the tributes started pouring in. The picture presented was that of a genuinely good guy, a friendly, happy fellow—an honest, honorable man who loved his job, his family, his faith, and the Buffalo Bills football team. Although he was a tough interviewer, he treated everyone with warmth and respect, from the city trash collector to the President of the United States.

In addition to being one of the great journalists of his time (*Time* magazine listed him as one of their "100 most influential people in the world" in 2008), Tim Russert was a person who strove to make the most of his considerable gifts while remaining true to who he was.

You could do a lot worse than following the example of Tim Russert. Be who you are, and be happy about it.

Two roads diverged in a wood, and I—
I took the one less traveled by,
And that has made all the difference.

—Robert Frost

"The Road Not Taken"

Lesson 87:
Set your own agenda.

I've attended a lot of meetings in my time, and led a lot of them too. One thing you need for a successful meeting is an agenda: a written list of the topics to be addressed and the order in which to address them.

When you have an agenda, your meeting generally flows smoothly. You can get a lot done in a reasonable amount of time because you know what has to be covered in the time available. Things don't always go exactly as planned, of course: sometimes you get off track, and some meetings can get rather contentious, but you usually get it back together and do what needs to be done.

If you try to run a meeting without an agenda, you have no idea what you're going to get. Topics come up from out of nowhere, and as often as not, you get sidetracked on unimportant matters. Usually, someone with a dominant personality will fill the leadership vacuum, often with disastrous results. When the gathering finally breaks up, everyone walks out wondering if they really accomplished anything.

If a *meeting* needs an agenda, a *life* needs one even more. As you make your way through adult life, you must set your own agenda. Here's an important bit of wisdom that you're likely to hear from several sources over the next few decades: If you don't set your own agenda, somebody else will.

You don't want someone else to set your agenda. I'm sure you can think of many instances where that has happened, and it's usually not pretty. The guy who enters the family business—not because he wants to, but because it's expected of him—and then proceeds to run the business into the ground while drinking away his troubles. The pretty young girl whose parents force her into beauty pageants even though she doesn't enjoy them. The physician who commits suicide because he never wanted to be a doctor— but did it to please his father.

Occasionally, the agenda that is set for you is a blank sheet of paper. Your boss doesn't think much of your abilities, so you get stuck in the same job for years or decades. In essence, your life goes nowhere.

Make your own agenda. Set a course for yourself. You might not get to the exact place you set out for, and there will surely be bumps along the way, but it'll be *your* trip. And I'll bet you can live with that.

Minds are like parachutes--they only function when open.

—Sir James Dewar

Lesson 88:
Keep an open mind.

You have a built-in advantage here. Young people are usually open-minded by nature; the trick is to stay that way as you age.

Politicians like to accuse one another of flip-flopping: changing positions on an important issue. A flip-flopper, the reasoning goes, is wishy-washy and indecisive, changing his mind just to please the shifting mood of voters. While this charge is sometimes true—it's no shock that a politician would pander for votes—it doesn't necessarily follow that changing one's mind is a bad thing.

Take George Wallace for example. While Governor of Alabama during the civil rights struggles of the 1960s, he famously stood on the steps of a University of Alabama building in a failed attempt to prevent the first black students from attending class. His battle cry of "segregation now, segregation tomorrow, segregation forever" came to symbolize opposition to equal rights for African Americans.

Through three terms as Governor of Alabama and three runs at the U.S. Presidency, George Wallace was the face of old-line racism in America. But George Wallace changed his mind.

In the early 1980s, he publicly announced that his long-held views on race had been wrong. He apologized to black civil rights leaders. They apparently took him at his word, because he was elected Governor for a fourth time in 1982, winning the support of most of the state's black voters. During that final term as Governor, he appointed a record number of blacks to state office.

You tell me: Is the George Wallace saga the story of a flip-flop—or the opening of a mind?

I think the argument can be made that nothing new can be accomplished without an open mind. The challenge is maintaining one as you grow older.

We each have our own lens through which we see the world. As we get older, we usually don't like to have that worldview threatened, so we tend to reject anything that doesn't fit. A closed mind can lead to a stale outlook and a grouchy disposition. An open mind gives you opportunities to learn and to appreciate other people and points of view. That can lead to a fresh outlook and sunny disposition. In short, an open mind can help keep you young.

*Riches are not from abundance of worldly
goods, but from a contented mind.*

—Mohammed

Lesson 89:
Be content, but never satisfied.

Warren Buffet is the richest man in the world. Depending on when you ask and who is doing the estimating, his fortune is valued at anywhere from $50 billion to over $62 billion. The guy has serious money.

Buffet is the perfect example of a self-made man. He started investing early. At age fifteen, he and a friend bought a used pinball machine for twenty-five dollars, which they placed in a barber shop for the customers to play. At twenty-six, he started an investment partnership company in his hometown of Omaha, Nebraska.

Over the next years and decades, Buffet became both rich and famous. His steady, commonsense approach to investing, along with his plain-talking style, earned him the nickname "The Oracle of Omaha." He's regarded by many observers as the greatest investor of the twentieth century.

Buffet bought his first home in 1958, when he was twenty-seven, paying $31,500 for a modest house in a middle-class Omaha neighborhood. Why is this important to our discussion? Because he's still there. As of this writing, he still lives in the same house over fifty years later. Inflation has increased its value to about $700,000, but it's no mansion.

Contrast the Buffet home with that of Bill Gates, the second-wealthiest person in the world by most counts. The Gates mansion was built in the 1990s on a lakeshore in Medina, Washington. According to Wikipedia.com (the source of all the statistical info on this page), the house has 50,000 square feet of floor space, twenty-five bathrooms, a dome-covered library, heated driveways, and an underwater music system for the pool. Its assessed tax value is $147 million—for a house!

Does this make Gates a bad guy? Not at all—he has a perfect right to spend his money as he sees fit. The point is that Buffet is happy with the life of a regular man. He shuns the trappings of wealth. Here's a guy who can afford to live anywhere in the world, yet he's content to stay in a home that is worth less than Bill Gates' annual property tax bill.

Warren Buffet is driven by the next challenge, whatever it may be—but he's also happy with who he is. He has achieved greatness without letting it go to his head. He is content, but never satisfied. May that be said of all of us.

If you must love your neighbor as yourself, it is at least as fair to love yourself as your neighbor.

—Sebastien-Roch Nicolas

Lesson 90:
Be your own best friend.

Have you ever heard the saying, "He's his own worst enemy"? This can be said of most of us, I suspect. But there's a flip side as well: you're also your own best friend.

You are the only person who has to live with yourself twenty-four hours a day, seven days a week, so if you don't like yourself, it's not going to be much fun. And because you only get one shot at life, it *should* be fun.

You are who you are. There's no getting around it. You can—and should—work to improve certain things about yourself. Maybe you talk too much, or maybe you don't talk enough. Maybe you need more patience or tolerance, a slower temper, or better driving habits. Maybe you need to learn to relax or accept criticism or not take things so personally.

Everybody has many areas that could use improvement, and you're no exception. But one thing is for sure: it's vitally important to like yourself. In fact, it's no exaggeration to say that you must love yourself unconditionally, just as you should love any other family member. If you can't honestly say that you do, then you should drop all other areas of self-improvement until you get this one fixed.

Think about that notion of yourself as your own best friend. Consider all the things you do for yourself: you feed yourself, dress yourself, bathe yourself, walk or drive yourself from one place to another, and keep yourself company all day and all night. You've gotta like a person who does all that stuff for you.

Here's how important it is. Consider the tragic case of Marilyn Monroe. She was America's most popular starlet in the 1950s and early '60s—and not just because of her looks and provocative roles. She was a genuinely talented actress. At the time of her death from apparent suicide in 1962, it seemed that everyone loved Marilyn except Marilyn—and nobody really knew why.

You need to maintain a close, healthy relationship with yourself. Like any other relationship, it will require time and effort to maintain. Take time for yourself. Exercise. Pursue a hobby that you enjoy. Relax with a good book. Go on a fun trip. When you're comfortable in your own skin, others will be comfortable in your presence. As the great Lucille Ball once said, "Love yourself first and everything else falls into line."

Energy is the essence of life.

—Oprah Winfrey

Lesson 91:
Whatever you do, do it with energy.

There is a secret to success in stage acting. If an actor knows and applies this secret, every performance will be a good one. It doesn't matter if he forgets a line or falls on his face, or if the scenery crumbles around him. If the actor applies this secret he will wow the audience every time the curtain rises.

Here's the secret: perform with energy. Energy is not something you can clearly describe, but people know it when they see it, and they also recognize when it's not present. A performance that lacks energy—even if it is otherwise perfect—will be seen by the audience as dull and even boring.

Why is this so? It's simple really. Energy is contagious. When an actor performs with a high level of energy, the audience feels its own energy level rise in a sort of sympathetic vibration. The performer in turn picks up on the audience's energy and feeds it back to them in a continuous, dynamic loop.

This principle applies to virtually everything you do in life. Energy is a personal force that comes from within you—and you control it. Whether you realize it or not, you decide how much energy to inject into every task.

Most people usually don't feel or display much energy. That's fine and normal, but it's rather dull and not much fun. By simply injecting energy into everything you do, you can improve your performance and sense of self-satisfaction.

One of my personal mottos is, "It doesn't take much to impress people." And it really doesn't. Mostly, all it takes is a little energy.

When you walk through a door, stride a little more purposefully. When you talk with someone, smile a little more enthusiastically. Listen a little more closely. Respond a little more earnestly. Be a little more interested in every task you perform, from the most mundane to the most important.

Don't fake it or force it, of course. Remember, energy comes from within; it's a natural force. Just tap in to that limitless reservoir of energy residing inside you. You'll be amazed at the difference.

We choose our joys and sorrows long
before we experience them.

—Kahlil Gibran

Lesson 92:
Have joy, joy, joy, joy down in your heart.

A friend of mine is the captain of his own charter sailboat in the Bahamas. Each week during charter season, which runs from March through August, Captain Bruce runs one-week charter voyages out of his base in Nassau. The groups that charter the *Bahama Star*, his fifty-three-foot sloop, run the gamut from church youth groups to corporate executives. The accommodations are less than luxurious (sort of like camping at sea), and the food, while tasty and plentiful, is by no means five-star cuisine.

Bruce and his wife Sheila share a so-called double bunk—which is about as wide as a twin bed. The bunk is located within five feet of the two heads—marine toilets—making for a less-than-fragrant resting place. That's okay, because Bruce doesn't get much sleep anyway. In addition to running the boat, he cooks the meals, maintains the boat and its diesel engine, and charts the daily course—all while closely monitoring the safety and enjoyment of his passengers.

Clearly, this is not the job for everyone. But Captain Bruce tackles it with a joy that is hard to resist. He obviously loves his life and enjoys every moment. He almost always has a smile on his face—not just a friendly smile, but a huge grin that comes from deep down inside.

He makes his passengers feel like family, because that's how he truly feels about them. His favorite expression of delight or surprise is a loud and hearty "AAARRRGGGGHHHHH!" that sends sympathetic vibrations to the top of the mast. Twenty-five years at sea have shaped him into a rough-hewn character that would be out of place in the country club dining room, but everyone who knows him loves him. His enthusiasm is so genuine and infectious that you can't spend much time around him without catching it yourself.

The story of Captain Bruce begs the question: is he joyful because he loves his work, or does he love his work because he's joyful? I suspect the answer is a combination of the two. But his joy clearly comes from within—it is a never-ending river that flows from a grateful heart and enriches everything it touches.

Joy allows us to see past the rough spots and appreciate the wonder of everything around us. It makes life a grand adventure. Tap into your own reservoir of joy, and see how grand life can be.

How desperately difficult it is to be honest with oneself.
It is much easier to be honest with other people.

—Edward White Benson

Lesson 93:
Don't kid yourself.

You know how we keep talking about your ability to control your own thoughts and attitudes? Well, this is the dark side of that concept.

Dishonesty requires two parties: one person telling the lie and the other believing the lie. The believer may believe because she has no reason not to—or perhaps because she wants to believe.

Victims of domestic abuse often fall into this category. The abuser feels remorse after beating his wife, so he promises never to do it again. Even though the victim has heard this particular lie many times before, and even though she has seen repeated evidence that he won't stop, she wants to believe him—and so she does.

In this case, the victim is buying into two lies: the one told by the abuser, and the one she tells to herself. She believes, even though she knows it's not in her interest to do so.

That's what makes it so hard to be honest with yourself—you want to believe the lie. If the victim were to be honest with herself, she would know the abuse will be repeated. With that clear understanding, she could seek some way to get out of her situation and begin the process of creating a new life.

Self-deception doesn't take place only in the context of abuse, of course. We fool ourselves all the time, in matters both big and small. Maybe you think you'll be able to complete five tasks in the next hour, when you'll really be lucky to complete two. You tell yourself that you have plenty of time to get ready for an appointment, and then you're surprised when you get there late. You think that you'd be truly happy if you could just get a new job or promotion.

You see, you have to use your ability of controlling your own thoughts judiciously, because it cuts both ways. You can use it for your benefit—in choosing your attitude, for example—or to your detriment. The trick is to recognize which is which.

Be candid with yourself. Ask yourself, "If I were an objective observer and knew everything I know, would I believe what I'm telling myself?" Then, as you answer, fight the urge to lie to yourself with your reply.

Maturity is a bitter disappointment for which no remedy exists, unless laughter could be said to remedy anything.

—Kurt Vonnegut, Jr.

Lesson 94:
Dang it, I've turned into my parents.

It happens to most of us, and you're probably no different. While you're growing up, your parents constantly try to influence your behavior by making little comments or lecturing you on various topics.

"Mind your manners." "Pick up after yourself." "Buckle your seat belt." "Show some respect." "Don't play with your food." It feels like they're going to drive you crazy; you've heard the same thing a thousand times. "Okay, okay," you say. "I get it already!"

Then one day—out of the blue—you hear yourself say something that your mother or father had said to you and that you swore to yourself you'd never use on anyone else. It's like an out-of-body experience. Where did that come from?

Ouch. Just like that, you've turned in to your parents.

First, allow me to extend my sympathies. You never intended for it to happen—in fact, you were probably determined *not* to let it happen. You're probably wondering where you went wrong.

You didn't go wrong, of course. This is just one of those little jokes nature plays on us. A lot of what we call maturation occurs when we aren't paying attention, and this is a great example of that phenomenon.

You don't really turn in to your parents—at least not completely. But our upbringing stays with us our entire lives, for better and for worse. Much of who we become is shaped by the teaching and example of parents. It's often impossible to deny or reject that influence, and you probably wouldn't want to.

Many hours have been spent on psychoanalysts' couches trying to make sense of parental influences—and in many cases trying to undo the accidental damage that they may have caused. As you're likely to discover for yourself, it's impossible to be a perfect parent. Remember, your parents are the products of their parents.

And understand that your parents did the best they could. Much of who you are is a product of their influence. That's not all bad.

*When a thing is done, it's done. Don't look
back. Look forward to your next objective.*

—Gen. George C. Marshall

Lesson 95:
No regrets.

Early on, we talked about the importance of not holding
a grudge. Regret is closely related to that concept, but it's
directed inward rather than toward others, and it's more a
feeling of sadness than anger. I think of it as a form of guilt.

You wish you had done a certain thing that you never
did, or that you had not done something that you did.
You keep reliving a certain moment of action or decision,
wishing you had acted differently.

Here's an example. In my business, I manage
investments for clients. By the time they find their way to
my office, they're usually over sixty and have been investing
for quite some time. That being the case, they of course
have an existing portfolio of investments.

A discussion with one new client—we'll call him
Jake—revealed that he had sold a particular stock years
ago that, had he held on to it, would have made him a
multimillionaire. To compound his woes, he had used the
proceeds from that sale to buy shares in a company that
quickly lost a great deal of its value.

As you might imagine, Jake constantly tortured himself over this event. "I can't believe how stupid I was," he would say. "Why didn't I just hang on to that stock?" Every time we talked, this sentiment would work its way in to the conversation.

What a waste of time, emotion, and mental energy. He was so preoccupied by these events that he couldn't bring himself to make a decision *now*—he was afraid of repeating what he had come to view as a tragedy.

Eventually I was able to convince him that he had simply made the best decisions he could with the information he had available at the time; that's all any of us can do. Maybe it works out, maybe it doesn't, but we've done our best. That's all you can expect.

No amount of thinking about it is going to change what happened in the past. Your life lies in the future—and that's a good thing, because you have the ability to influence the future. You can do nothing about the past. Leave it behind you. You'll make plenty of mistakes in your lifetime, but don't concern yourself with them. Walk boldly ahead.

The wise man must remember that while he is a descendant of the past, he is a parent of the future.

—Herbert Spencer

Lesson 96:
Always look ahead.

You may have heard the philosophy, "Live for the moment." The thinking goes something like this: yesterday is gone, tomorrow is not guaranteed, so live for today.

Although it sounds good, it's not a very practical way to live your life. I think the logic breaks down in the notion that tomorrow is not guaranteed to us. That may be true as far as it goes, but it is a very short-sighted philosophy.

Sure, there are no guarantees in life, but there is a very high likelihood that you will live to see tomorrow, and the day after that, and many, many more days after that.

In other words, there's a good chance you'll live a long, long time, so you'd better be doing everything you can now to improve the quality of your future life.

Life is a continuous series of "here-and-now" moments. This current moment, during which you're reading this page, is one. All those moments that led up until now were, in their time, here-and-now moments. And each of the remaining moments in your life will be its own here-and-now moment.

Many of your here-and-now moments are spontaneous, seemingly unrelated to anything that has gone before. But how you think and act *now* can have a profound impact on the quality of many of those future moments.

Many older people have learned this concept, because they have lived a long time. They could tell you that if you want to retire comfortably, you need to save now. If you want to be healthy and active twenty years from now, you need to eat healthy and exercise now. If you want to be able to look back on a life that was worth living, you need to live in a way that enriches the lives of others.

But even more important, you must have some unachieved goal or dream to reach for in order to give meaning to your present as well as your future. Keep pushing. Keep reaching. Keep looking ahead and moving ahead. It will give meaning to your life, and your here-and-now moments will be all the sweeter for it.

Gratitude is the healthiest of all human emotions.

—Zig Ziglar

Lesson 97:
Give thanks in all things.

Have you ever noticed that things don't always turn out the way you expect them to? Life is *hard*.

So what can you do about it? You can feel sorry for yourself, complain, or wish that things had turned out differently—in short, you can focus on the negative. Or you can have what has been called an "attitude of gratitude."

Think you've got it bad? Life is no picnic, sure, but it's no harder for you than it is for most. Look at the world around you and you'll see hunger, violence, disease, injustice, and poverty—misery on a scale you and I can only imagine.

Instead of focusing on what you don't have, what you can't do, or what didn't work out, spend some time focusing on what you do have.

Even though we don't know each other, I'll make these guesses about you: You live in a country where you can make your own choices about where to live, what to think and believe, and what career to pursue. You have a brain that's at least as good as most. Your judgment and maturity qualify you as an adult. You probably have a roof over your head and probably know where your next meal is coming from. You have at least a few friends or family members who care about you. If you find yourself in a job you don't like, you could—if you really wanted to—quit and try something else.

So what are you whining about?

Everybody has problems, and everybody has blessings. You can count your problems or count your blessings. Start by counting your blessings.

Thank those people who have made your life better. Allow yourself to appreciate the opportunities you have, the resources you have, the friends you have—in short, the life you have. If you keep counting, you might just run out of time to count your problems.

If you think about it, I'll bet you really have a lot to be thankful for. Live each moment of each day in the full knowledge of that truth.

*Only in quiet waters do things mirror
themselves undistorted. Only in a quiet mind
is adequate perception of the world.*

—Hans Margolius

Lesson 98:
Nurture yourself.

Your value to the outside world is based more on your behavior than your thoughts, feelings, and attitudes. But those thoughts, feelings, and attitudes are vital, because they influence your behavior and help determine your level of happiness. Let's review the concepts discussed in this final section.

It is essential to be happy with who you are. Inner turmoil drains a lot of effort and energy that could otherwise be applied to more important pursuits (Lesson 86). Set your own agenda. If you don't, someone else will, and you probably won't like it (87). As you grow older, work hard to retain the open-mindedness of youth (88).

Learn to be content with who you are, where you are, and what you have—but never be satisfied. Contentedness gives you peace of mind, while dissatisfaction spurs you on to bigger and better things (89). Your self-image should actually go beyond contentment to real appreciation. You are your own constant companion, your own best friend.

Learn to like yourself as a person; believe in yourself, and do it with feeling (90).

Inject as much energy as you can into everything you do. It will boost your performance and make life more fun (91). Live each day with a sense of joy so that you can look beyond the rough spots to the beauty of life (92).

It's easy to deceive yourself—easier, perhaps, than deceiving others—but the consequences of self-deception can be catastrophic. Work hard to honest with yourself at all times (93). There may well come a day when you find yourself acting like your parents. Try not to be alarmed; it doesn't mean that you'll be just like them, and it's not necessarily a bad thing to borrow a bit from Mom and Dad occasionally (94).

We close with these very important thoughts. Your life lies in the future. The past cannot be changed, so don't relive past mistakes or decisions (95). Instead, look boldly ahead toward a bright future—a future over which you can exercise a great deal of control (96). And as you travel through life, take time to give thanks for all that you have been given and for the marvelous opportunities you have (97).

In the final analysis, life is all about choices. It can be a grand adventure—if you choose to make it so. And with the right choices, you can leave the world better off than you found it.

Something tells me that you're going to be just fine.

We are not human beings having a spiritual experience.
We are spiritual beings having a human experience.

—Pierre Teilhard de Chardin

Lesson 99:
Assume your place.

Throughout this book, we've talked about your place within the world. We've talked about the fact that you have the awesome power to shape your own destiny. We've said that success and happiness lie not in looking inward, but in focusing outside of yourself. We've established the certainty that it's a wonderful life. You also know that you'll encounter serious problems, heartaches, and probably even tragedy, and that you have the ability to handle it all.

In short, this is a huge world, loaded with joy and troubles. And you have the power to establish your own special place within it. In this incredible, infinite universe, you *fit* —just perfectly.

They say no man is an island. That's true, you know. You are an ever-changing, ever-growing piece an intricate puzzle, and your individual identity is created not in isolation but as part of the whole. Each living being combines with other living beings, so that the great wide world is in itself a massive living thing, which in turn is just a small part of the great universe beyond. And you are a very important part of it all.

If all this is true, then it's no stretch to say that there is a spiritual connection among all things. The fact that you occupy that unique place makes you a spiritual being, whether you realize it or not.

There are many religions in the world, each of which was founded as a way to understand that spiritual connection. In this context, religion is not just a way of explaining our differences, but of explaining what binds us together.

Egyptian novelist Alaa Al Aswany says, "Religions...are a way to find God, a way to have positive values, to prove oneself as a good human being. You feel God in your heart, you feel God when you love others." And, it can be added, you feel God when you make your place in the world, and make the world a better place for your having been here.

Go forth. Make your way. Know that life is good. And know that, whatever comes your way, you have your own special place in this wonderful, wonderful world.

About the author

Andrew Millard has extensive experience in education and personal advising. A former teacher and high school principal, he is co-owner and Investment Advisor Principal for Main Street Financial Group, an insurance and investment advisory firm. His first book, *Low-Stress Investing: 10 Simple Steps to a Worry-Free Portfolio*, was a finalist for the Benjamin Franklin Book Award for Best New Voice Nonfiction. He has degrees from Presbyterian College and Wake Forest University, and he holds the Certified Financial Planner™ designation. A frequent guest speaker for various civic, professional, and student groups, he also has won numerous awards and recognition for his community involvement. His hobbies include travel, photography, golf, public speaking, and singing. He lives in western North Carolina with his wife; they have a grown son.

Discover more lessons—and add your own—at:

www.wisegraduate.com

BUY A SHARE OF THE FUTURE IN YOUR COMMUNITY

These certificates make great holiday, graduation and birthday gifts that can be personalized with the recipient's name. The cost of one S.H.A.R.E. or one square foot is $54.17. The personalized certificate is suitable for framing and

will state the number of shares purchased and the amount of each share, as well as the recipient's name. The home that you participate in "building" will last for many years and will continue to grow in value.

THIS CERTIFIES THAT
YOUR NAME HERE
HAS INVESTED IN A HOME FOR A DESERVING FAMILY

1985-2005
TWENTY YEARS OF BUILDING FUTURES IN OUR
COMMUNITY ONE HOME AT A TIME

1200 SQUARE FOOT HOUSE @ $65,000 = $54.17 PER SQUARE FOOT
This certificate represents a tax deductible donation. It has no cash value.

Here is a sample SHARE certificate:

YES, I WOULD LIKE TO HELP!

I support the work that Habitat for Humanity does and I want to be part of the excitement! As a donor, I will receive periodic updates on your construction activities but, more importantly, I know my gift will help a family in our community realize the dream of homeownership. **I would like to SHARE in your efforts against substandard housing in my community!** *(Please print below)*

PLEASE SEND ME _____ SHARES at $54.17 EACH = $ $_____

In Honor Of: _____

Occasion: (Circle One)   HOLIDAY   BIRTHDAY   ANNIVERSARY
         OTHER: _____

Address of Recipient: _____

Gift From: _____   *Donor Address:* _____

Donor Email: _____

I AM ENCLOSING A CHECK FOR $ $_____ PAYABLE TO HABITAT FOR HUMANITY **OR** PLEASE CHARGE MY VISA OR MASTERCARD *(CIRCLE ONE)*

Card Number _____ Expiration Date: _____

Name as it appears on Credit Card _____ Charge Amount $ _____

Signature _____

Billing Address _____

Telephone # Day _____ Eve _____

PLEASE NOTE: Your contribution is tax-deductible to the fullest extent allowed by law.
Habitat for Humanity • P.O. Box 1443 • Newport News, VA 23601 • 757-596-5553
www.HelpHabitatforHumanity.org

Printed in the United States
140942LV00001B/1/P